ASL
American Sign Language

Literature Series

Bird of a Different Feather

&

For a Decent Living

TEACHER'S GUIDE

SAM SUPALLA & BEN BAHAN

American Sign Language Literature Series
Series Editors: BEN BAHAN, SAM SUPALLA

ISBN 0-915035-21-9

_____ **FOR ORDERING INFORMATION:** _____

To purchase the *American Sign Language Literature* Teacher's Set, please contact:

DawnSignPress
9080 Activity Road–Suite A
San Diego, California 92126

(619) 549-5330 V/TTY (619)549-2200 FAX

• • •

This series is dedicated to
our deaf parents

Clarence and Patricia Supalla
Eleanor and James V. Bahan

for all the stories
they have told us
and that we can now
tell the world.

• • •

TABLE OF CONTENTS

Bird of a Different Feather

For a Decent Living

For a Decent Living

ACKNOWLEDGMENTS

THE ORIGINS of the *American Sign Language Literature Series* date back to 1986 in a coffeehouse in Berkeley, California. The idea was conceived over several cups of stiff, black coffee. That coffeehouse dream turned into an arduous seven years of research, development and production. The combined efforts of many talented and able people led to the initial release of the *ASL Literature Series*, which we believe adds significantly to the literary heritage of the deaf community.

DawnSignPress was instrumental in financing this project, which took place at the University of Arizona and Boston University. Along the course of development, numerous people at both sites contributed to help make this work a reality, and we thank all these individuals wholeheartedly.

In their efforts with research and development, the following people have contributed significantly to each step of production: data transcription and analysis, videotape production, typing, consulting, assisting in the development, and editing of the guide: *Debbie Aarons, Todd Czubek, Jeff Davis, Martha B. Dayton, Janey Greenwald, Rosemarie Jones, Carla Ketelhut, Chris Orminston, Mary Jane Pollisco, Sherill Rogers, Robin Supalla, David Wagenknecht, Pat Wagenknecht, Melinda Weinrib, Cathy Wilson and Tina Wix.*

For field-testing materials and offering constructive feedback in the polishing of the final product, we would like to thank: *Steve Nover and Cindy Volk from the University of Arizona's Sign Language/Deaf Studies Program and the students of Boston University's Deaf Studies and Deaf Education Program: Spring 1992.*

We are indebted to our wives, who provided moral support and encouraged us along the way, even at times when the end seemed like an eternal mirage: *Robin Supalla and Sue Burnes.* An added note of appreciation goes to *Robin Supalla* who helped a great deal in organizing the editorial content of the Teacher's Guide.

Not least of all, we must thank *Joe Dannis,* our publisher, for his ongoing support over the past seven years. Also deserving recognition is the DawnSignPress Production Staff: *Tina Jo Breindel, Marla Hatrak, Stacey Lawson, Iosep MacDougall, Robin Mitchell and Lynn Stafford,* all of whom worked days and nights to help complete the materials.

• • •

INTRODUCTION

THE *American Sign Language Literature Series* is an innovative and exciting resource for teaching American Sign Language (ASL) as a foreign language. As you may well be aware, literature is a vital component of any foreign language curriculum and provides an excellent medium for studying culture. Although ASL lacks a conventional writing system, this does not mean that the deaf community in the United States has no oral version of literature.

Orality serves as an effective medium for many cultures around the world, and the same holds true for the deaf community. The narrative form of ASL ranges from anecdotes to full-length stories. The two ASL narratives presented belong to the category of full-length stories. They were originally developed by the Signers that you see in the videotape. Signer with a capitalized "S" indicates a person who is an accomplished oral literary artist and has performed in front of large audiences. The Signers that you see in these ASL narratives are among the few who have achieved national recognition for their work.

The two narratives targeted for study through the *ASL Literature Series* are *Bird of a Different Feather* and *For a Decent Living*. The *ASL Literature Series* serves advanced students who are learning ASL as a foreign language. This text would be appropriate for students studying at approximately the fourth level of ASL courses.

Students studying ASL as a foreign language need to expose themselves to the life and experiences of deaf people. These narratives reveal insights into the culture of the deaf community. Narratives are not only for pleasure but serve a valuable teaching function. Deaf people rely on ASL narratives to portray themselves and reaffirm their identities as members of a distinct cultural group. Therefore, narratives serve as an effective medium for the cultural component of ASL as a foreign language instruction.

Orality is another component of ASL literature that students can appreciate. Students need to understand how a narrative is formed without a writing system, and how ASL narratives are developed and how they are maintained based solely by memory. Students' natural desire to follow a story facilitates the learning process as well as the development of both comprehension and expressive skills specific to the narrative form.

You should spend a minimum of one hour each week in class teaching ASL literature; however, you will need to establish your own timetable depending on your teaching style and the length and schedule of your course.

Each student needs to purchase a student package containing a Student Videotext and Student Workbook. You should familiarize yourself with these materials. In the Student Videotext, the two narratives are divided into segments of various levels. The Student Workbook is based on the videotext. Students will need to view the narratives and complete a comprehension check before scheduled class sessions. They should also review both the linguistic and cultural background information presented in the workbook. To achieve a balance between in-class and out-of-class activities, your students' homework assignments will be followed by an in-class discussion of literary questions under your guidance. You should provide personal anecdotes related to the narratives. Finally, assign students to retell certain segments of both narratives in order to enhance their expressive skills as well.

There are three videotaped renditions of *Bird of a Different Feather* and *For a Decent Living*. One videotape, the Collector's Edition, is designed for collection purposes. The other two are used for study–one for your use in the classroom and the other for student use outside the classroom. The Collector's Edition includes both narratives shown in full. The Teacher's Videotape and Student Videotext have broken the narratives down into segments. Students will rely on their version to study the narrative and to help prepare them for the class discussion. Also, a videotaped interview with the Signers is included in the Teacher's Videotape. The interviews are to be shown in class to help students develop a deeper understanding of the narratives based on their origins and development.

The Teacher's Guide is broken down into two major components: General Overview and Lesson Plans. These components are followed by a set of appendices consisting of transparency masters for use in the classroom. The organization of the Teacher's Guide will allow you to better understand the presentation of the narrative for the purpose of study as well as all relevant components of the *ASL Literature Series* used both in and out of the classroom. Each Lesson Plan begins with a synopsis of events in the narrative. The synopsis is followed by a list of materials and equipment needed in the classroom. A set of instructional steps is also provided to help guide you through the analysis of the two narratives. The instructor's package consists of the Teacher's Guide, Student Workbook and all three versions of the videotape.

We believe that the *ASL Literature Series* will enhance your existing curriculum and contribute to your students' appreciation of the role of literature in the deaf community.

• • •

ASL NARRATIVE ORGANIZATION

THE TWO NARRATIVES in the *ASL Literature Series* are divided into segments to maximize their instructional value. Each narrative is divided into parts, chapters, topic units, and strophes, as indicated in the following chart.

The narrative *Bird of a Different Feather* is comprised of two parts, "The Mountain" and "The Valley." This narrative begins with Chapter 1, "The Eggs," and ends with Chapter 9, "The Flight." Furthermore, Chapter 1 is comprised of two topic units and strophes 1-13. You will gain a greater understanding of what constitutes each segment type after viewing the Student Videotext, since the Teacher's Videotape is broken down into chapters only.

The following chart will help you visualize the relationship between the segments in each narrative. Each Lesson Plan covers one chapter section of the chart, which acts as a synopsis of the narrative structural organization.

ASL NARRATIVE BREAKDOWN

Bird of a Different Feather

Part 1 THE MOUNTAIN

CHAPTER 1 THE EGGS		CHAPTER 2 SEARCH FOR A CURE				CHAPTER 3 THE SCHOOL YEARS		
Topic Unit		Topic Unit				Topic Unit		
1 The Family	2 The Doctor	3 The Source	4 The Faith Healer	5 The Medicine Man	6 The Doctors	7 The School Philosophy	8 The Lessons	9 The Ambition
Strophes		Strophes				Strophes		
1-8	9-13	14-15	16-21	22-26	27-32	33-37	38-42	43-48

CHAPTER 4 VOCATIONAL TRAINING			CHAPTER 5 OUT IN THE WORLD		
Topic Unit			Topic Unit		
10 The Flying Lesson	11 The Hunting Lesson	12 Evaluation for Graduation	13 Preparation for Hunting	14 Finding Prey	15 Bird's Future Considered
Strophes			Strophes		
49-53	54-59	60-62	63-64	65-69	70-76

Bird of a Different Feather

Part 2 THE VALLEY

For a Decent Living

• • •

INSTRUCTIONAL PREPARATION

THE *ASL Literature Series* Teacher's Guide is a user-friendly manual designed to help you prepare and conduct your lessons. It includes a Lesson Plan for each chapter of both narratives. These plans include steps to follow with in-class activities and homework assignments.

The *ASL Literature Series* has eight components:

- Comprehension Check
- Language Notes
- Background
- Literary Questions
- Anecdotal Sample
- Retelling
- Interview with Signer
- Examination/Grading

As you may well be aware, students often lack study in both the comprehension and cultural background areas when studying ASL narratives. With the *ASL Literature Series*, however, the homework assignments (i.e., using the Student Videotext to accompany the Student Workbook) are designed to provide support in these areas as well as cover the linguistic aspects of ASL narratives. The information covered in the student homework assignments will allow a study of the narratives in greater depth involving a form of literary analysis. The *ASL Literature Series* also maximizes the use of class time for certain activities related to literary analysis, personal anecdotes, and retelling. The basic prerequisite for students studying *Bird of a Different Feather* and *For a Decent Living* lies in their full comprehension of both narratives.

With the **Comprehension Check**, students view the narrative in the Student Videotext strophe by strophe and answer questions in the Student Workbook. Students bring their completed assignment to the next scheduled class session. In class, they exchange their workbooks and correct each other's assignments. You need to provide the answer key on an overhead transparency. Students additionally learn by correcting and discussing their errors. Students provide examples of errors and offer an explanation as to why they believe it was answered incorrectly. If time does not permit for every student in your class to comment, you can pick just a few. You should note any error patterns and elaborate on them in class in order to prevent them from reoccuring.

Language Notes are also in most of the strophes studied in the Comprehension Check. Each language note includes a still picture of the Signer producing a sign, followed by text describing the target sign and role play. This component of the *ASL Literature Series* is expected to provide students with direct exposure on how role play operates in ASL marking either the orientation of narrator or character. Both eye gaze and body shifting behaviors of the Signers are clearly illustrated in the still pictures.

After the students complete each chapter, they will need to read the **Background** section. The background section contains cultural information related to the chapter. The background sections occur after most chapters in the student workbook and allow students to learn more about the cultural significance of the events.

The last component of the Student Workbook is **Literary Questions**. The literary questions aim at involving students in describing the characters and events in the chapter. Students write short answers to the questions prior to the class session and hand them to you during class. You should evaluate these papers based on effort and clarity of answers. Students' homework assignment on the questions prepares them for further discussion in class.

In class, students should be divided into either three or four groups (depending on the number of literary questions) and be shown the literary questions to discuss. Prior to the discussion, you will need to show the Teacher's Videotape of the chapter; recall that until now, students have studied the chapter only by individual strophes, and they need to view the narrative segment at the chapter level. After the student discussion, one leader from each group should present their answer to one of the questions to the class.

In the Lesson Plan, you will find a general answer guide to the literary questions. Keeping in mind that there are no "right" or "wrong" answers, you should elicit discussion between groups about each others' answers. Be sure to share some of your answers or insights with the class as well.

The literary questions are based on a formal literary analysis of the two narratives. These questions are designed to direct students' attention to the depth of the narratives and provide them with insights on how characters and events reflect the culture of the deaf community.

The **Anecdotal Sample** is a vital component of the *ASL Literature Series*. You are encouraged to read the anecdotal sample provided in the Lesson Plan and tell them to your students. You may want to use the samples as a guide in recollecting your own experiences. Your personal experiences may impact students, as they see how the narrative mirrors real lives. More importantly, students will learn that anecdotes are another narrative form critical for sharing cultural information. Students are encouraged to participate with their own anecdotes, since sharing anecdotes promotes an interaction which will further develop both their receptive and expressive ASL skills.

The **Retelling** component remains a critical element of the *ASL Literature Series*. For students, retelling a narrative promotes their incidental and almost unconscious learning. "Linguistic spillover" describes this learning process whereby there is an anticipated reappearance of certain ASL linguistic forms, structures and concepts in students' signed production after the retelling sessions.

There are three retelling assignments in each narrative. Each retelling assignment is detailed in the corresponding Lesson Plan. In general, there is a retelling assignment at the strophe, topic unit, and chapter level for each narrative. Students need to first practice their retelling assignment out of class with their Student Videotext. The retelling procedure is "oral to oral" with each student reciting the particular segment as told by the Signer for the first assignment. Retelling does not mean that students need to imitate "word for word" what they have viewed on videotape. Rather, the retold segment can be of any style, as long as the storyline remains intact.

The first retelling event assigns all students strophes to retell in consecutive order (i.e., Strophe 1, Strophe 2, Strophe 3, etc.) in front of the class while being videotaped. You should replay the videotape immediately and allow students to view their completed retelling assignment, as feedback will allow students to improve their performance for the next time. Grades are not given for strophe-level retelling assignments. Grading begins with the topic unit-level assignment. At the topic unit level, students will be videotaped individually and in private. You will evaluate the videotaped topic unit retelling assignment out of class using the Narrative Retelling Evaluation form provided. This form is designed to help you with targets and criteria for evaluation, and you will need to include written feedback as well. The final retelling assignment will be at the chapter level (again videotaped individually and in private) and will allow students to be creative in developing their own endings to the narrative. It is suggested that you choose several of the most creative endings to share with the class. The retelling assignments and procedures as described here are the same for both narratives.

At the end of each narrative, the Lesson Plan instructs you to show the **Interview with Signer** provided in the Teacher's Videotape. Students are expected to ask questions about the interview to promote comprehension before they do a two-page reaction paper. In reading the reaction papers, you should look for interesting remarks made by students and share these during the next class session.

Examination/Grading includes three written examinations. These should be administered according to the time frame specified in the Lesson Plan. Basically, the areas covered in the examinations will be a review of the Backgrounds, Language Notes and Literary Questions. Sample questions are given for each of three examinations. We feel that these sample questions would appropriately test this material. However, you should feel free to develop your own questions as well.

Grading student participation is encouraged. You should keep track of students' workbook work and their in-class comprehension checking and discussions as well as their reaction papers. You should also record their participation in the retelling assignments at the strophe level. Students' sharing of personal anecdotes or asking questions related to your anecdotal telling should also be taken into consideration for grading.

We propose, as an example, grading the *ASL Literature Series* at 30% of your curriculum. Thus, if you specify a total of 150 points for the *ASL Literature Series* in the course syllabus, the detailed breakdown for your grading and evaluation would be as on the following page:

Retelling   (Total: 40 points)
- Topic unit level, 2 sessions (5 points each)
- Chapter level, 2 sessions (15 points each)

Examinations   (Total: 90 points)
- Part level, 1 exam (30 points)
- Narrative level, 2 exams (30 points each)

Participation   (Total: 20 points)
- Comprehension Check
- Retelling at strophe level
- Literary discussion
- Reaction paper to Interview with Signer
- Sharing own anecdotes with class

The following are suggested readings related to ASL literature and orality:

Bahan, B. (1992). American Sign Language Literature: Inside the Story. In J. Mann (Ed.), *Deaf Studies What's Up Conference Proceedings*. Washington DC: Gallaudet University, College for Continuing Education.

Bahan, B. & Supalla, S. (in press). Line Segmentation and Narrative Structure: A Study of Eye Gaze Behavior in American Sign Language. In K. Emmorey & J. Reilly (Eds.), *Sign, Gesture and Space*. Hillsdale, NJ: Lawrence Erlbaum Associates, Inc.

Edwards, V. & Sienkewicz, T. (1990). *Oral Cultures Past and Present: Rappin' and Homer.* Cambridge, MA: Basil Blackwell.

Frishberg, N. (1992). Signer of Tales: The Case for Literary Status of an Unwritten Language. *Sign Language Studies*, 59, 149-170.

Gee, J. (1992). A Linguistic Approach to Narrative. *Journal of Narrative and Life History, 1* (1), 15-39.

McMahon, E., Funk, R., & Day, S. (1988). *The Elements of Writing About Literature and Film.* New York, NY: MacMillan Publishing Company.

Supalla, S. & Bahan, B. (1992). American Sign Language Literature Series: Research and Development. In J. Mann (Ed.), *Deaf Studies for Educators Conference Proceedings* (pp.137-149). Washington DC: Gallaudet University, College for Continuing Education.

TEACHING HINTS

- View the Collector's Edition, Teacher's Videotape and Student Videotext to familiarize yourself with the varying formats.

- Read through the Student Workbook to familiarize yourself with its components.

- Note the approximate time allocations indicated in the Lesson Plan activities. These are provided as a guide to help you in preparing for each class session. Decide how you will use a course time frame prior to beginning a lesson.

- Read through the Teacher's Guide and be sure you understand the terminology presented in "Literary Questions." To assist you in this, we recommend highly that you read the handbook, *The Elements of Writing About Literature and Film* listed in the recommended readings. Consider including this handbook as an optional material for students.

- Make transparencies of all appendices prior to the course. File in a notebook to be used as needed.

- Note equipment needed prior to scheduled class sessions.

- Specify your expectations and grading methods for the *ASL Literature Series* in your course syllabus.

• • •

Bird of a Different Feather

INTRODUCTORY LESSON PLAN

MATERIALS/EQUIPMENT NEEDED

- Collector's Edition videotape
- VCR/Monitor

INSTRUCTIONAL STEPS

1. INTRODUCTION   **35 minutes**
- Introduce students to the *ASL Literature Series*.
- Show Collector's Edition of *Bird of a Different Feather* in full.

2. HOMEWORK ASSIGNMENT
- Students complete Chapter 1, "The Eggs."

TOTAL TIME ALLOTTED TO INTRODUCTION: *35 minutes*

Lesson Plan 1

CHAPTER 1
THE EGGS

Topic Unit	
1 The Family	2 The Doctor

Strophes	
1-8	**9-13**

Synopsis

Mama and Papa Eagle are anxiously awaiting the hatching of their four eggs. Three "normal" eaglets hatch and the parents are thrilled. They await the arrival of their fourth eaglet. Their excitement turns into shock and disappointment as the fourth baby bird emerges with a long, straight beak, and not a normal, curved, eagle-like beak. The stunned parents summon the doctor, who confirms their suspicions: the fourth baby bird does indeed have a "defective" straight beak. The doctor informs the parents that the baby bird is too young to undergo treatment, but the parents should visit him again in six months. When the doctor leaves, the parents blame each other for causing the deformity. They resolve their argument by remembering that they have three other normal eaglets.

MATERIALS/EQUIPMENT NEEDED

- Teacher's Videotape
- Appendix 1: Comprehension Check Answer Key/Chapter 1
- Appendix 1a: Literary Questions/Chapter 1
- Overhead projector
- VCR/Monitor

INSTRUCTIONAL STEPS

1. HOMEWORK
- Collect Literary Question answers.

2. COMPREHENSION CHECK   **15 minutes**
- Students exchange workbooks.
- Note students who have not completed assignment.
- Display overhead of Comprehension Check Answer Key.
- Students correct each others' answers.
- Students offer explanations for incorrect answers.
- Note any error patterns and address them.

3. LITERARY QUESTIONS   **25 minutes**
- Review Teacher's Videotape, Chapter 1.
- Divide class into four groups.
- Display overhead of Literary Questions.
- Each group discusses one question.
- One leader from each group reports their answer to the class.
- Class discussion of answers.
- Respond based on guide below.

LITERARY QUESTION GUIDE

1. The doctor makes a house call, which is uncommon. The family has four children (eaglets), which is also uncommon. The parental roles seem very divided. It is suggested that the story occurred during the baby boom era (i.e., 1950s).

2. Since you cannot hear the beak, the doctor's decision to use the stethoscope shows the posturing of the medical profession. Doctors try to look like they know what they are doing at all times. The irony of listening to a beak seems to reflect the medical profession in general.

3. Mama and Papa Eagle blame each other for Straight Beak's beak, although they do not know what caused it. They rationalize their feelings by emphasizing the fact that they have three "normal" eaglets. The parents never really resolve the conflict over who was responsible for the beak, although they did end their argument.

4. Curved-beak eagles represent hearing people and people with power. For example, the eagle doctor represents someone with power. Straight Beak represents someone without power. This parallels the deaf experience where Straight Beak represents deaf people. Also, many hearing parents can identify with the identification process that the Eagle parents went through: they find out their child is deaf; they argue and blame each other.

---

4. ANECDOTE   **10 minutes**
- Ask class if anyone has a deaf relative. If so, ask them to elaborate.
- Provide anecdote from below or share your own relevant to the identification of deaf children (e.g., how your parents may have reacted to your deafness, if applicable).
- Students ask questions related to anecdote.

ANECDOTAL SAMPLE

One deaf couple was pretty sure that their baby was deaf. They conducted the standard home-tests, like clapping behind the baby, etc. Although the baby did not seem to respond to the various noises, the parents were not grief-stricken. They assumed the deafness was hereditary. Anyway, they took the baby for a formal hearing test, where the doctor "apologetically" informed them that their baby was indeed deaf. The parents smiled at each other and then thanked the doctor. The doctor stared and asked if he could help answer questions or provide information, but the deaf couple was just content to know their child was like them – deaf.

---

5. NEW HOMEWORK ASSIGNMENT
   • Students to complete Chapter 2, "Search for a Cure."

TOTAL APPROX. TIME ALLOTTED TO CHAPTER 1:   *50 minutes*

Lesson Plan 2

CHAPTER 2			
SEARCH FOR A CURE			
Topic Unit			
3 The Source	4 The Faith Healer	5 The Medicine Man	6 The Doctors
Strophes			
14-15	16-21	22-26	27-32

Synopsis

Rather than wait six months, the parents try to find a cure for their deformed eaglet on their own. They read in the Enquirer about a healing priest who can cure deformed and crippled birds. They bring Straight Beak to the priest who tries to heal him in the church by praying to God. When all his efforts fail, the priest tells the family to read the Bible and trust God so that Straight Beak will be healed. Next, the family takes Straight Beak to a Native American medicine man. The medicine man concocts a potion and performs a ritual dance that is supposed to cure Straight Beak, but it does not work. The medicine man says that they should take the potion home and feed it to Straight Beak three times a day. That does not work either. Finally, after six months, they bring Straight Beak back to the doctor who diagnosed him. The doctor re-examines Straight Beak and announces that their only option is surgery. However, the operation is costly and they are unable to find someone who can perform the operation at a reduced rate. The parents' last visit is to an Ear, Nose and Throat Specialist (E.N.T.) who explains that there is another option: a special school that turns straight-beaked birds into eagles. The parents are ecstatic over this option.

MATERIALS/EQUIPMENT NEEDED

- Teacher's Videotape
- Appendix 2: Comprehension Check Answer Key/Chapter 2
- Appendix 2a: Literary Questions/Chapter 2
- Overhead projector
- VCR/Monitor

INSTRUCTIONAL STEPS

1. HOMEWORK
- Collect Literary Question answers.

2. COMPREHENSION CHECK   15 minutes
   • Students exchange workbooks.
   • Note students who have not completed assignment.
   • Display overhead of Comprehension Check Answer Key.
   • Students correct each others' answers.
   • Students offer explanations for incorrect answers.
   • Note any error patterns and address them.

3. LITERARY QUESTIONS   25 minutes
   • Review Teacher's Videotape, Chapter 2.
   • Divide class into four groups.
   • Display overhead of Literary Questions.
   • Each group discusses questions.
   • One leader from each group reports their answer to one question to the class.
   • Class discussion of answers.

LITERARY QUESTION GUIDE

1. Straight Beak is viewed as a problem that needs to be fixed. Due to his "illness," Straight Beak is taken all over town in attempts to treat him. The underlying thought is that the eagles are "right" and something is "wrong" with Straight Beak.

2. Mama Eagle is concerned enough to take Straight Beak everywhere in search of a cure, instead of waiting the six months as instructed by the doctor. Mama Eagle is obviously more desperate than she is patient.

3. The Signer implies that the parents have refused to accept the fact that one of their offspring has a straight beak. The Signer takes the narrator's role in telling the audience that the parents have not yet accepted this.

4. Sending Straight Beak to school is a temporary resolution: "out of sight, out of mind." The parents are not faced with Straight Beak on a daily basis. Therefore, Straight Beak's placement in the school provides a temporary solution for the parents.

---

4. ANECDOTE   10 minutes
   • Provide anecdote from below or share your own relevant to the idea of "curing" deafness.
   • Students ask questions related to anecdote.

ANECDOTAL SAMPLE

There was a young deaf boy whose parents took him many places in search of a cure for his deafness. One place they took him was a roadside campsite led by a "spiritual healer." They brought the boy there and the healer began chanting and pounding his hands over the boy's ears. It hurt the boy. After the first time, the healer realized the boy was still deaf, so he pounded on his ears a second, third, and fourth time! In incredible pain, the boy finally said "Yes" to the healer, meaning that he could hear, so the healer would stop. Proudly, the healer announced to the boy's mother that the boy was cured. The mother cried tears of joy and put the boy in the car to go home. On the drive home, it was evident, however, that he was still deaf.

5. NEW HOMEWORK ASSIGNMENTS
• Students to complete Chapter 3, "The School Years."
• Assign one strophe per student for retelling.

TOTAL TIME ALLOTTED TO CHAPTER 2:   *50 minutes*

Lesson Plan 3

CHAPTER 3		
THE SCHOOL YEARS		
Topic Unit		
7 The School Philosophy	8 The Lessons	9 The Ambition
Strophes		
33-37	38-42	43-48

Synopsis

Upon arriving at the special school, Straight Beak and his mother meet with the principal, a highly trained specialist in straight-beak education. He explains the school's philosophy to them. The principal explains that if the straight-beaked birds practice hard enough and think long enough, they will indeed become normal, curved-beak eagles. Straight Beak joins a classroom where they practice beak-bending and wing-stretching exercises based on the principle that, since they are young and flexible, it will be easy to change their beaks into curved beaks and their wings into strong wings. Straight Beak is left at the school and his mother goes back home. Upon entering high school, the teacher has the class write down their future vocational aspirations. When the teacher reads that most of the class aspires to be mere birds, she becomes furious and bawls them out! The teacher explains that the birds are eagles and beyond those low-life goals. She says they must all aspire to become hunters like all eagles.

MATERIALS/EQUIPMENT NEEDED

- Teacher's Videotape
- Appendix 3: Comprehension Check Answer Key/Chapter 3
- Appendix 3a: Literary Questons/Chapter 3
- Overhead projector
- VCR/Monitor
- Video camera
- Blank videotape

INSTRUCTIONAL STEPS

1. HOMEWORK
- Collect Literary Question answers.

2. RETELLING ACTIVITY   45 minutes
- Set up video camera.
- Begin taping with student retelling Strophe 1 in front of class.
- Continue taping students signing strophes, in order, until completed.
- Show their completed, signed version of the strophes immediately.
- Provide individual feedback as each strophe is signed.

3. COMPREHENSION CHECK   15 minutes
- Students exchange workbooks.
- Note students who have not completed the assignment.
- Display overhead of Comprehension Check Answer Key.
- Students correct each others' answers.
- Students offer explanations for incorrect answers.
- Note any error patterns and address them.

4. LITERARY QUESTIONS   25 minutes
- Review Teacher's Videotape, Chapter 3.
- Divide class into four groups.
- Display overhead of Literary Questions.
- Each group discusses questions.
- One leader from each group reports their answer to one question to the class.
- Class discussion of answers.

LITERARY QUESTION GUIDE

1. The A. G. Beak Association symbolizes the A. G. Bell Association for the Deaf. Both strive toward the goal of "fixing" problems. The principal's plaque qualifies him with authority and history because it is associated with a professional association. The meaning behind this is that surely the principal will be able to "fix" Straight Beak's problem.

2. The first part of the question is open-ended.

   At this point in the story, Mama Eagle is desperate after many failed attempts to cure Straight Beak by the doctor, the preacher and the medicine man. Mama Eagle feels open to suggestions to solve the problem. Mama Eagle seems relieved that the school seems to understand her plight and that the school promises to make an eagle out of Straight Beak. She believes in them.

3. The birds' aspirations were not within the accepted limits of what an eagle should become. The birds must learn to follow the traditions of the eagle. Hunting represents the only way of life for the straight-beaked birds. This is equivalent to manual labor. Although in the narrative, eagles become doctors, principals and preachers, the best the straight-beaked birds can hope for is to do manual labor.

(continued)

(continued)

4. The wing-stretching and beak-bending exercises are equivalent to oral/speech training therapy for deaf children. Moreover, the classroom is managed in an orderly fashion–turn taking at carefully planned exercises. This is like an oral deaf classroom. Also, the teacher in the narrative is always in control and gives commands with no real open flow of communication between the teacher and students. Again, this is similar to the interaction in many deaf classrooms with a non-signing teacher.

5. ANECDOTE   10 minutes
   • Provide anecdote from below or share your own relevant to speech training (e.g., how you endured speech lessons, if applicable) with your class.
   • Students ask questions related to anecdote.

ANECDOTAL SAMPLE

There was a 10-year-old girl in a residential school for the deaf. She was practicing one of the first words she planned to say in public, "Coke®." She practiced and practiced C-O-K-E, trying to remember that the 'E' was silent and how to correctly pronounce the 'C' and 'K' sounds. One weekend, the girl rode the bus home from school and transferred buses at the bus station. This particular bus station had a soda fountain where she planned to speak the one word she had been practicing so diligently, "Coke." Her heart was pounding, she was so nervous! After practicing in her head another ten times how to pronounce "Coke," she sat down at the counter and the waitress approached her. The girl looked her straight in the eyes and said "Coke." The waitress just stared and did not move. After a few seconds she bowed her head in closer. The girl realized that her speech had "failed" and so she tried again, a little louder this time, to be sure that the waitress could hear her... "Coke!" Unfortunately, she spoke so loudly that all the customers at the counter turned and stared at her and the waitress even jumped a little. The girl was completely humiliated and scrambled for a pen and piece of paper. Totally embarrassed, she wrote down "Coke" and handed the paper to the waitress. It was her first time trying to speak a word in public, and she had failed.

6. NEW HOMEWORK ASSIGNMENT
   • Students to complete Chapter 4, "Vocational Training."

TOTAL APPROX. TIME ALLOTTED TO CHAPTER 3:   *95 minutes*

Lesson Plan 4

CHAPTER 4		
VOCATIONAL TRAINING		
Topic Unit		
10	11	12
The Flying Lesson	The Hunting Lesson	Evaluation for Graduation
Strophes		
49-53	54-59	60-62

Synopsis

The students go to Vocational Training to learn how to hunt. They are taught several important steps to succeed in hunting. First, they learn the head-tilt, to zero in on the target. Also they learn advanced flying skills. After these steps are mastered, the birds are taught to dive by throwing their wings back and diving towards the target. The birds are then taught to right themselves in order to grab hold of the target and carry it off. Although the last steps are not fully mastered, the teacher commends the class in their efforts. After much hard work and practice, graduation day finally arrives. The students and their families were so happy that no one noticed they were all still straight-beaked.

MATERIALS/EQUIPMENT NEEDED

- Teacher's Videotape
- Appendix 4: Comprehension Check Answer Key/Chapter 4
- Appendix 4a: Literary Questions/Chapter 4
- Overhead projector
- VCR/Monitor

INSTRUCTIONAL STEPS

1. HOMEWORK
- Collect Literary Question answers.

2. COMPREHENSION CHECK   15 minutes
- Students exchange workbooks.
- Note students who have not completed assignment.
- Display overhead of Comprehension Check Answer Key.
- Students correct each others' answers.
- Students offer explanations for incorrect answers.
- Note any error patterns and address them.

3. LITERARY QUESTIONS   25 minutes

- Review Teacher's Videotape, Chapter 4.
- Divide class into four groups.
- Display overhead of Literary Questions.
- Each group discusses questions.
- One leader from each group reports their answer to one question to the class.
- Class discussion of answers.

LITERARY QUESTION GUIDE

1. Placement in the vocational track implies that Straight Beak is incapable of becoming a high achiever. It establishes Straight Beak on a career path of manual labor. In today's standards, this would be the equivalent of menial duties. If Straight Beak had been placed in the academic track, he may have gone to college and become whatever he had chosen.

2. Ironically, the teacher praised Straight Beak because he did the best he could do as a straight-beaked bird. However, he was only being praised for his *effort*, which does not necessarily translate into his skill.

3. The educational philosophy led Straight Beak to believe that he could succeed, even though he was physically incapable of performing the task. Therefore, the educational philosophy set Straight Beak up for failure.

4. Just as a high school diploma does not assure that "Johnny" can read, the birds' diplomas show only that the birds learned how to behave like eagles, not that they had become eagles. Similarly, speech training may help deaf people gain same access to the hearing world, although it does not make them a part of that world.

---

4. ANECDOTE   10 minutes

- Provide anecdote from below or share your own with the class.
- Students ask questions related to anecdote.

ANECDOTAL SAMPLE

There was a girl in a deaf school who could not speak, although she signed very well. When they screened her for placement in the school, they placed her in the manual track. Even though she had aspirations of going to college, the principal and her teachers told her she could not. She was disappointed when they placed her in vocational training, but she chose to major in childcare. Upon high school graduation, she entered the job market and found a job in childcare. She continued working in childcare with mostly hearing individuals. She was a very smart woman and all her co-workers questioned her as to why she did not go to college. She told them she could not because her teachers and principal said she could not (because she could not talk). They encouraged her to take the Gallaudet placement exam and so she did. She passed the test and graduated from Gallaudet University and then went on to get a Master's and a job in a big city as a social worker counseling and encouraging deaf children to go to college.

5. NEW HOMEWORK ASSIGNMENT
- Students to complete Chapter 5, "Out in the World."
- Announce examination date covering Part 1 of the narrative.
  (Exam can be given any time after completion of Chapter 5; see Appendix 5b: Model Examination Sample #1)

TOTAL APPROX. TIME ALLOTTED TO CHAPTER 4:   *50 minutes*

Lesson Plan 5

CHAPTER 5		
OUT IN THE WORLD		
Topic Unit		
13	14	15
Preparation for Hunting	Finding Prey	Bird's Future Considered
Strophes		
63-64	65-69	70-76

Synopsis

When Straight Beak arrives home with his family, they look at his diploma and notice that his specialization was hunting. They make plans to go hunting the next morning. At 4:00 a.m., Straight Beak joins his father and three burly eagle brothers to go hunting. When the first target, a rabbit, is spotted, the family gives Straight Beak the honors. Straight Beak applies all that he has learned in vocational training–the head tilt, the dive, and finally, righting himself in order to clamp down on the rabbit. The rabbit feels something on his back and tries to swat the annoyance away. Straight Beak, unable to carry off the rabbit because of its weight, tries to convince the rabbit to go with him voluntarily. The rabbit offers Straight Beak his carrot which Straight Beak carries off to his family. At that moment, the father realizes that his son is not independent. The family returns home. Papa Eagle explains what happened to Mama Eagle and expresses concern that someone would have to take care of Straight Beak for the rest of his life. The parents ask the three brothers if they would be willing to take care of their bird brother when the parents die. The brothers agree. Thus Straight Beak's future is dictated by the rest of the family while Straight Beak unknowingly sits and watches television in another room.

MATERIALS/EQUIPMENT NEEDED

- Teacher's Videotape
- Appendix 5: Comprehension Check Answer Key/Chapter 5
- Appendix 5a: Literary Questions/Chapter 5
- Overhead projector
- VCR/Monitor

INSTRUCTIONAL STEPS

1. HOMEWORK
- Collect Literary Question answers.

2. COMPREHENSION CHECK   15 minutes
- Students exchange workbooks.
- Note students who have not completed assignments.
- Display overhead of Comprehension Check Answer Key.
- Students correct each others' answers.
- Students offer explanations for incorrect answers.
- Note any error patterns and address them.

3. LITERARY QUESTIONS   25 minutes
- Review Teacher's Videotape, Chapter 5.
- Divide class into four groups.
- Display overhead of Literary Questions.
- Each group discusses questions.
- One leader from each group reports their answer to one question to the class.
- Class discussion of answers.

LITERARY QUESTION GUIDE

1. Straight Beak's pleading with the rabbit tells us that he knows his own limitations.

2. The incident renewed their concerns for Straight Beak's future because they never fully resolved the original conflict raised during his infancy. Also, their discussion about Straight Beak with their other children passes down their concern to another generation of family members.

3. It is assumed that Straight Beak is incapable of independence and therefore must depend on others for his survival. Thus Straight Beak becomes a burden to the entire family.

4. Straight Beak's identity has not developed much in Part One. His identity is defined by how others view him. However, he did show a little about himself in arguing with the rabbit. Even so, the argument shows that he knows his limitations, which have been defined by others.

---

4. NEW HOMEWORK ASSIGNMENTS

- Students to complete Chapter 6, "The Bird World."
- Assign one topic unit per student for retelling. If more than 15 students, feel free to assign the same topic unit to more than one student.

TOTAL TIME ALLOTTED TO CHAPTER 5: *40 minutes*

Lesson Plan 6

CHAPTER 6		
THE BIRD WORLD		
Topic Unit		
16	17	18
Family Moves to a New Land	Singing in the Valley	Berries in the Valley
Strophes		
77-82	83-90	91-97

Synopsis

One day Papa Eagle makes the announcement that he has found a new home for the family. The home is far away, with lots of animals and plenty of food. The family sends off their belongings in a storage truck and begins the long flight to their new home. As they are flying, Straight Beak falls further and further behind because it takes ten of his wing flaps to travel the same distance as one curved-beak eagle wing flap. He becomes exhausted and is unable to notify his family of his condition. Straight Beak looks for a place to rest and can only see the forbidden valley below. He lands on a tree branch in the valley and hears a bird singing on the other side of the tree. Straight Beak acts repulsed by this sound, since he was taught to think this way in school. Straight Beak confronts the singing bird about his singing, but then Straight Beak is reluctantly challenged into trying to sing himself. Straight Beak begins to sing and for the first time in his life he feels free to be himself. He is so grateful to the singing bird that he offers to find food for him. Once again, his hunting techniques fail and the squirrel gets away. The singing bird introduces berries to Straight Beak, and once again Straight Beak is appalled. After hesitating for a moment, Straight Beak tastes and then devours all the berries he can eat. He has a wonderful afternoon mingling in the valley with his new-found friends.

MATERIALS/EQUIPMENT NEEDED

- Teacher's Videotape
- Appendix 6: Comprehension Check Answer Key/Chapter 6
- Appendix 6a: Literary Questions/Chapter 6
- Overhead projector
- VCR/Monitor
- Video camera(s)
- Blank videotape(s)

INSTRUCTIONAL STEPS

1. HOMEWORK
- Collect Literary Question answers.

2. RETELLING ACTIVITY   **45 minutes**
- Set up video camera.
- Begin taping students one at a time in a separate room (or two at a time with two cameras) until all students have completed the topic unit assignment.
- Evaluate students' retelling after class using Narrative Retelling Evaluation form (Appendix 6b).

3. COMPREHENSION CHECK   **15 minutes**
- Students exchange workbooks.
- Note students who have not completed assignment.
- Display overhead of Comprehension Check Answer Key.
- Students correct each others' answers.
- Students offer explanations for incorrect answers.
- Note any error patterns and address them.

4. LITERARY QUESTIONS   **25 minutes**
- Review Teacher's Videotape, Chapter 6.
- Divide class into four groups.
- Display overhead of Literary Questions.
- Each group discusses questions.
- One leader from each group reports their answer to one question to the class.
- Class discussion of answers.

LITERARY QUESTION GUIDE

1. The valley symbolizes the deaf world. Singing symbolizes signing. Eating berries symbolizes cultural socialization.

2. Internalized oppression learned at school and at home from his family explains his resistance to participate in the bird world.

3. Straight Beak never really had the opportunity to express himself or interact with his peers until he entered the bird world. There he finally had the opportunity to set himself free by learning the language of birds, which became a vehicle of expression. This was a language in which Straight Beak could set himself free.

(continued)

(continued)

4. Straight Beak's oppression and learned values have surfaced and prevented him from acculturating with the rest of the birds. Similarly, many deaf people are raised learning hearing values and not being exposed to deaf values as well. Deaf people need to learn deaf values. That way, they develop a sense of pride in who they are and in their language. This makes it easier for them to acculturate with others.

5. ANECDOTE   10 minutes
   • Provide anecdote from below or share your own (e.g., perhaps you know of someone who was formerly an oral deaf person and is now signing) with the class.
   • Students ask questions related to anecdote.

ANECDOTAL SAMPLE

One deaf person had a very hard time acculturating into the deaf community. This man was raised in a hearing family and was constantly told not to stare, because it is not polite. However, since he was deaf, his eyes compensated for his ears, and he had to really work at not staring at people. He had to become good at lip reading while not really staring at the person–a pretty difficult task. After many years of practice, he perfected that special skill of glancing at and then looking away from people, so as not to be impolite. Upon entering the deaf world, he quickly was labeled "snobbish," because most deaf people assumed that he was not interested in what they had to say, since he constantly looked away from them as they talked. It seems that successful acculturation is a continual process, because even after many years of immersion in the deaf community, he still has to work on appropriate eye-gaze behavior.

6. NEW HOMEWORK ASSIGNMENT
   • Students to complete Chapter 7, "Return to the Eagle World."

TOTAL APPROX. TIME ALLOTTED TO CHAPTER 6:   *95 minutes*

Lesson Plan 7

**CHAPTER 7
RETURN
TO EAGLE WORLD**

Topic Unit	
19	20
Eagle Mother Returns	Back to the Eagle World

Strophes

| 98-100 | 101-104 |

Synopsis

Suddenly an eagle is spotted flying overhead. All the birds run for cover except for Straight Beak, who welcomes his mother. Mama Eagle bawls him out for disappearing and being in the forbidden valley, and they fly home together. At home, Straight Beak is punished and sent to his room. While eating dinner, the family hears a strange noise coming from Straight Beak's room. Papa Eagle enters the room and finds Straight Beak singing! Papa Eagle is outraged. He forbids Straight Beak to sing like a low-life bird and reminds him that he must always act like an eagle. After time and constant immersion in the eagle world, Straight Beak eventually assimilates back into the eagle world.

MATERIALS/EQUIPMENT NEEDED

- Teacher's Videotape
- Appendix 7: Comprehension Check Answer Key/Chapter 7
- Appendix 7a: Literary Questions/Chapter 7
- Overhead projector
- VCR/Monitor

INSTRUCTIONAL STEPS

1. HOMEWORK
- Collect Literary Question answers.

2. COMPREHENSION CHECK   15 minutes
- Students exchange workbooks.
- Note students who have not completed assignment.
- Display overhead of Comprehension Check Answer Key.
- Students correct each others' answers.
- Students offer explanations for incorrect answers.
- Note any error patterns and address them.

3. LITERARY QUESTIONS   25 minutes
- Review Teacher's Videotape, Chapter 7.
- Divide class into four groups.
- Display overhead of Literary Questions.
- Each group discusses questions.
- One leader from each group reports their answer to one question to the class.
- Class discussion of answers.

LITERARY QUESTION GUIDE

1. It means that Straight Beak is back to his old way of life. This does not imply happiness for Straight Beak.

2. The birds' reaction of fear shows the power of the eagles in the bird world. However, to Straight Beak, the eagle is his mother.

3. Straight Beak's self-identity increased slightly when he showed that he enjoyed singing, even though singing is considered taboo in the eagle world. His obvious enjoyment of singing and eating berries shows that he has begun to develop his true self.

4. Papa Eagle's reaction shows that he is still in denial and has not yet accepted Straight Beak for who he is. Papa Eagle has denied Straight Beak his own friends and life and has demanded that he behaves like an eagle.

---

4. ANECDOTE   10 minutes
- Provide anecdote from below or share your own (e.g., how some deaf people are kept at home with their parents or relatives throughout adulthood) with the class.
- Students ask questions related to anecdote.

ANECDOTAL SAMPLE

One president of a local deaf club shared the story with his friends about how every year at Christmas, one deaf man would always show up for the annual Christmas party. He would just stand and stare at the people talking all night long. He would only participate in brief conversations. Mostly, he just stared and watched everyone else. He seemed to be taking in as much as possible, and he really seemed to enjoy himself, although he rarely shared anything about himself. One year after the party was over and the president was locking up the club, he found the man still standing there. Only after the president encouraged him to go home did he explain that his car had fallen into a ditch a few miles down the road on his way to the party, and

(continued)

(continued)

he was stranded. In disbelief, the president followed the man's directions and drove to the sight where the car had fallen. Sure enough, buried under a mound of snow, they found the car. The president was beside himself and asked why he did not mention this sooner. The man explained how important it was to him to be around other deaf people and signing once a year. It seems that the man's father only let him have use of the car once a year at Christmas time, so he could go to the deaf club party. The man did not want to waste precious time worrying about his car, because his annual social event was much more important to him. The president later learned that the man's father held him down to working on the family farm.

5. NEW HOMEWORK ASSIGNMENT
• Students to complete Chapter 8, "The Operation."

TOTAL APPROX. TIME ALLOTTED TO CHAPTER 7:   *50 minutes*

Lesson Plan 8

CHAPTER 8		
THE OPERATION		
Topic Unit		
21 The News	22 The Cure	23 The Eagle Feast
Strophes		
105-107	108-111	112-114

Synopsis

One day Mama and Papa Eagle arrive home with good news. They have found a doctor who can perform an operation on Straight Beak's beak to make it eagle-like. With coaxing from his family, Straight Beak agrees to undergo the operation so that he can be "normal." When Straight Beak awakens after the operation, he finds his beak bandaged and his family standing around his bed, teary-eyed. The doctor unwraps his beak and the family is ecstatic to see that he now has a typical eagle beak. A party is thrown in celebration of Straight Beak's new look. There are many eagles at the party exclaiming how wonderful he looks, but Straight Beak overhears some kids mocking him and calling him a parrot. Mama Eagle encourages him to ignore the remarks, but Straight Beak cannot help but wonder about his identity now. Mama Eagle asks if he wants some roasted pig, but he can only think of the delicious berries he enjoyed back in the valley. Straight Beak declines the offer and decides that he needs some rest instead.

MATERIALS/EQUIPMENT NEEDED

- Teacher's Videotape
- Appendix 8: Comprehension Check Answer Key/Chapter 8
- Appendix 8a: Literary Questions/Chapter 8
- Overhead projector
- VCR/Monitor

INSTRUCTIONAL STEPS

1. HOMEWORK
- Collect Literary Question answers.

2. COMPREHENSION CHECK   **15 minutes**
- Students exchange workbooks.
- Note students who have not completed assignment.
- Display overhead of Comprehension Check Answer Key.
- Students correct each others' answers.
- Students offer explanations for incorrect answers.
- Note any error patterns and address them.

3. LITERARY QUESTIONS   25 minutes
  - Review Teacher's Videotape, Chapter 8.
  - Divide class into four groups.
  - Display overhead of Literary Questions.
  - Each group discusses questions.
  - One leader from each group reports their answer to one question to the class.
  - Class discussion of answers.

LITERARY QUESTION GUIDE

1. It implies that they do not accept Straight Beak for who he is, and they are still looking for a way to cure or change him. Their decision about Straight Beak's happiness is based solely on their own view of happiness. It does not take into account Straight Beak's feelings.

2. Children generally are more truthful and less tactful. Adults tend to try and "save face" and not make waves. Therefore, they tend to agree with each other in this type of situation, which could be potentially embarrassing.

3. The parrot symbolizes "close, but no cigar," meaning that Straight Beak looks the part of an eagle and is a good imitation, but he is not the real thing. Note that parrots tend to imitate human speech, although they do not understand what is being said.

4. Often times, when children see their parents under duress, they feel compelled to relieve this duress and make them happy, especially if the children feel that they are a contributing factor of the unhappy feelings. One major limitation of the cochlear implant is that it cannot be reversed. However, the patient does not necessarily become a hearing person, and the social implications have not been fully researched.

---

4. NEW HOMEWORK ASSIGNMENTS
  - Students to complete Chapter 9, "The Flight."
  - Assign retelling at the chapter level. Students create and retell Chapter 9 with a new ending for the narrative.
  - Announce date for Examination #2, which covers the entire narrative.
    (Exam can be given any time after completion of Chapter 9; see Appendix 9b: Model Examination Sample #2)

TOTAL APPROX. ALLOTTED TIME TO CHAPTER 8:   *40 minutes*

Lesson Plan 9

CHAPTER 9			
THE FLIGHT			
Topic Unit			
24	25	26	27
Return to the Valley	Ejected from the Choir	The Berry Struggle	The Flight into Sunset
Strophes			
115-117	118-121	122-124	125-126

Synopsis

The next morning Straight Beak awakens with a craving for the delicious berries, so he tells Mama Eagle that he's going out for a while and sneaks back to the forbidden valley. When the valley birds see Straight Beak's beak, they question him about it. Not wanting to boast now that he is part of the superior eagle world, he lies and tells them he flew into a window. The valley birds express their sympathy and invite him to join in the choir. The conductor detects some odd noises, and after testing the birds individually, he determines that the noises are coming from Straight Beak and his new eagle beak. Straight Beak is ejected from the choir and disappointedly sits and hums to himself. Later, the birds go for berries and Straight Beak is once again disappointed as he realizes that he cannot grab and eat berries with his new curved eagle beak. He watches the birds singing and eating berries, and looks back to the eagle world and then into the sunset. He flies off into the sunset, realizing that he does not belong in either world.

MATERIALS/EQUIPMENT NEEDED

- Teacher's Videotape
- Appendix 9: Comprehension Check Answer Key/Chapter 9
- Appendix 9a: Literary Questions/Chapter 9
- Overhead projector
- Video camera(s)
- Blank videotape(s)
- VCR/Monitor

INSTRUCTIONAL STEPS

1. HOMEWORK
- Collect Literary Question answers.

2. RETELLING   **45 minutes**
- Set up video camera.
- Begin taping students one at a time in a separate room (or two at a time with two cameras) until all students have completed the chapter level assignment.
- Evaluate students' retelling after class using Narrative Retelling Evaluation form (Appendix 6b).

3. COMPREHENSION CHECK   **15 minutes**
- Students exchange workbooks.
- Note students who have not completed assignment.
- Display overhead of Comprehension Check Answer Key.
- Students correct each others' answers.
- Students offer explanations for incorrect answers.
- Note any error patterns and address them.

4. QUESTIONS FOR DISCUSSION   **25 minutes**
- Review Teacher's Videotape, Chapter 9.
- Divide class into three groups.
- Display overhead of Literary Questions.
- Groups discuss one question.
- One leader from each group reports their answer to one question to the class.
- Class discussion of answers.

LITERARY QUESTION GUIDE

1. This tells us that Straight Beak himself is ambivalent or marginal, and not sure of what he wants.

2. Straight Beak decides that he does not belong to either world and that perhaps he needs to start a new life someplace else.

3. In Part Two, Straight Beak experiences a new life style, even though he is still not strong enough to develop his own identity. Lack of strong identity is why he accepted the operation. In the end, Straight Beak realizes it is too late to reverse the operation and understands that he is neither a bird nor an eagle. He needs a place to belong. His decision to fly off is the first and last decision he makes for himself in the narrative.

---

5. INTERVIEW WITH SIGNER   **25 minutes**
- Show Interview with the Signer in Teacher Videotape.

6. NEW HOMEWORK ASSIGNMENTS
- Students to write a two-page reaction paper based on the Interview with the Signer.
- Students to complete Chapter 1, "Living on the Farm," in the ASL narrative, *For a Decent Living*.

TOTAL APPROX. TIME ALLOTTED FOR CHAPTER 9: 110 minutes

For a Decent Living

INTRODUCTORY LESSON PLAN

MATERIALS/EQUIPMENT NEEDED

- Collector's Edition videotape
- VCR/Monitor

INSTRUCTIONAL STEPS

1. INTRODUCTION   **20 minutes**
- Show Collector's Edition of *For a Decent Living*.

2. HOMEWORK ASSIGNMENT
- Students to complete Chapter 1, "Living on the Farm."

TOTAL TIME ALLOTTED TO INTRODUCTION: *20 minutes*

Lesson Plan 10

CHAPTER 1

LIVING ON THE FARM

Topic Unit	
1 The Farm Family	2 Incident in the Barn
Strophes	
1-4	**5-9**

Synopsis

A cold and snowy blizzard-like farm scene is depicted. A boy is seen sitting and painting in a room, when suddenly his drunken father bursts into the room and confronts him. The boy knows what his father wants–for him to go and do work in the barn. After his father and mother quarrel, the boy sadly puts away his treasured painting supplies and bundles up to brave the cold walk to the barn. Upon entering the barn, the boy notices that his father had used his paintings to cover up the broken windows. The boy becomes enraged and runs off into the night.

MATERIALS/EQUIPMENT NEEDED

- Teacher's Videotape
- Appendix 10: Comprehension Check Answer Key/Chapter 1
- Appendix 10a: Literary Questions/Chapter 1
- Overhead projector
- VCR/Monitor

INSTRUCTIONAL STEPS

1. HOMEWORK
- Collect Literary Question answers.

2. COMPREHENSION CHECK   15 minutes
- Students exchange workbooks.
- Note students who have not completed assignment.
- Display overhead of Comprehension Check Answer Key.
- Students correct each others' answers.
- Students offer explanations for incorrect answers.
- Note any error patterns and address them.

3. LITERARY QUESTIONS   25 minutes
- Review Teacher's Videotape, Chapter 1.
- Divide class into four groups.
- Display overhead of Literary Questions.
- Each group discusses questions.
- One leader from each group reports their answer to one question to the class.
- Class discussion of answers.

LITERARY QUESTION GUIDE

1. Outside is a sense of vastness. The cold blizzard snow provides a mood of desolation. One gets the sense of being lonely and alone in the cold world. Inside the house is warm, but there is still a sense of desolation.

2. Their communication has broken down. The father knows that his son is deaf, but he makes no effort to communicate with him visually. This inability to communicate could be due, in part, to the father's drinking problem. However, with no attempt at communicating except for pointing/gesturing, the boy follows through with the request to avoid a potential conflict with his father.

3. Painting represents a quiet but visual way in which the boy can express himself to his family and the world around him. However, since the father does not hold value in painting, he does not seem to hold value for the boy.

4. The question is open-ended.

---

4. ANECDOTE   10 minutes
- Ask class the questions, "Where do you think the protagonist learned to sign?" and "Why do you think he did not sign to his parents?"
- Provide anecdote from below or share your own relevant to the experience that many deaf children have in learning signed language (e.g., from deaf parents or through peer interaction at residential schools).
- Students ask questions related to anecdote.

ANECDOTAL SAMPLE

A deaf boy with deaf parents was enrolled in a residential school for the deaf when he was about six years old. In the dorm where he slept, the older kids would always come to talk and play with him. He was popular with the older kids because American Sign Language (ASL) was his native language and he communicated well with them. However, the boy's classmates were left alone because they did not know how to sign. Most of these kids just knew their own home sign systems from their hearing families. It was interesting because, as the boy socialized with the older kids (who had spent the last few years learning ASL), no one tried to teach or encourage the non-signers to sign. But one girl would just stand and watch the signing all day long. She never tried to join in; she would just stare and watch the boy and his friends playing and talking. It was an amazing transformation because after just one month of watching, the girl began signing, too! She had absorbed the language just by being exposed to it for one short month. After that, many other classmates had learned ASL, too.

---

5. NEW HOMEWORK ASSIGNMENT
• Students to complete Chapter 2, "Moving to the City."

TOTAL APPROX. TIME ALLOTTED TO CHAPTER 1: 50 minutes

Lesson Plan 11

CHAPTER 2
MOVING TO THE CITY

Topic Unit	
3	4
Meeting the Deaf Peddler	Finding the Deaf Club

Strophes

10-14	15-16

Synopsis

The boy arrives in the busy city and, after exploring, he unexpectedly meets a deaf peddler. After getting the address of the local deaf club, the boy rides the trolley there.

MATERIALS/EQUIPMENT NEEDED

- Teacher's Videotape
- Appendix 11: Comprehension Check Answer Key/Chapter 2
- Appendix 11a: Literary Questions/Chapter 2
- Overhead projector
- VCR/Monitor

INSTRUCTIONAL STEPS

1. HOMEWORK
- Collect Literary Question answers.

2. COMPREHENSION CHECK   15 minutes
- Students exchange workbooks.
- Note students who have not completed assignment.
- Display overhead of Comprehension Check Answer Key.
- Students correct each others' answers.
- Students offer explanations for incorrect answers.
- Note any error patterns and address them.

3. LITERARY QUESTIONS   25 minutes
- Review Teacher's Videotape, Chapter 2.
- Divide class into four groups.
- Display overhead of Literary Questions.
- Each group discusses questions.
- One leader from each group reports their answer to one question to the class.
- Class discussion of answers.

LITERARY QUESTION GUIDE

1. The city itself is bustling and full of life, in contrast to the quiet, solitary, cold, isolated farmland. The boy feels the same in both places: isolated and alone.

2. The boy feels comfortable in the fact that he can control the pace of his exploring. The shop windows are not as busy and bustling as the city streets. It is also possible that the boy feels a connection to the mannequins; behind their glass walls, they have their own quiet world, just as the boy may feel a wall between himself and the outside hearing world.

3. The peddler represents the boy's connection to the deaf world and his subsequent connection to deaf friends, so the boy's contact with the peddler is important. Being from the farm, the boy may not carry a stigma towards the peddler.

4. The question is open-ended.

4. ANECDOTE   **10 minutes**
   • Ask class if they have met a deaf peddler, and if so, ask them to elaborate.
   • Provide anecdote from below or share your own relevant to peddling.
   • Students ask questions related to anecdote.

ANECDOTAL SAMPLE

One day a deaf girl answered the door and a man was standing there and handed her an "ABC" peddling card. The deaf girl was young and assumed the man was hearing, so she went into the other room and gave her deaf father the card. Her father took one look at the card and immediately jumped up and grabbed his shotgun. He ran to the door and aimed the gun at the peddler, who took off in a puff of smoke! The little girl was shocked until her father explained that the man was a door-to-door deaf peddler. What angered her father most was that the peddler reflected negatively on the reputation of deaf people.

5. NEW HOMEWORK ASSIGNMENT
   • Students to complete Chapter 3, "Visiting the Deaf Club."

TOTAL APPROX. TIME ALLOTTED TO CHAPTER 2:   *50 minutes*

Lesson Plan 12

Synopsis

After finding the deaf club, the boy meets an older man formerly from the same residential school for the deaf as himself. This man introduces the boy to the president of the club. During this meeting, the boy learns about potential job prospects in the area. One prospect that catches his attention is at the aircraft factory, although a deaf person had never been hired there before. The boy waves to the peddler he had met earlier. The president interprets this exchange as a friendship between the two, thus suspecting that the boy was actually a peddler himself. The boy is immediately expelled from the club and finds refuge with the man who originally introduced him to the president.

MATERIALS/EQUIPMENT NEEDED

- Teacher's Videotape
- Appendix 12: Comprehension Check Answer Key/Chapter 3
- Appendix 12a: Literary Questions/Chapter 3
- Overhead projector
- VCR/Monitor

INSTRUCTIONAL STEPS

1. HOMEWORK
- Collect Literary Question answers.

2. COMPREHENSION CHECK   15 minutes
- Students exchange workbooks.
- Note students who have not completed assignment.
- Display overhead of Comprehension Check Answer Key.
- Students correct each others' answers.
- Students offer explanations for incorrect answers.
- Note any error patterns and address them.

3. LITERARY QUESTIONS   **25 minutes**
- Review Teacher's Videotape, Chapter 3.
- Divide class into four groups.
- Display overhead of Literary Questions.
- Each group discusses questions.
- One leader from each group reports their answer to one question to the class.
- Class discussion of answers.

LITERARY QUESTION GUIDE

1. The hallway is quiet, dark, long, and lifeless. In contrast, the clubroom is loud, bright, crowded and full of life.

2. The questions posed were particular to the introductory discourse of deaf culture. The questions also serve as a gatekeeping process to the culture. The doorman takes on the role of gatekeeper.

3. The big, burly president has an overpowering presence. The boy's reluctance to meet the president is a reflection of the boy's lack of self–confidence, due in part to his wish to be accepted and not rejected (i.e., like with his father) again.

4. The manner in which the boy presented himself, as eager to get a job, conflicts with his association with the peddler. This conflict could suggest that the boy had another agenda. Thus, he is perceived as lying about wanting to get a job. The peddler's role, however, is clear.

---

4. NEW HOMEWORK ASSIGNMENTS
- Students to complete Chapter 4, "Getting a Job."
- Assign one strophe per student for retelling.

TOTAL TIME ALLOTTED TO CHAPTER 3:   *40 minutes*

Lesson Plan 13

CHAPTER 4				
GETTING A JOB				
Topic Unit				
8	9	10	11	12
The Aircraft Factory	The Job Request	A Job Found	In the Factory	The Good Worker
Strophes				
30-31	32-37	38-40	41-44	45-47

Synopsis

The next morning, the boy resolves to get a job at the aircraft factory. His first visit is unsuccessful, but his persistence in returning daily to the aircraft factory finally lands him a job on an assembly line. His boss is nice and shows him how to do the assembly work. The boss even knows how to fingerspell. The boy's performance at the factory is excellent, but he is lonely as the sole deaf employee.

MATERIALS/EQUIPMENT NEEDED

- Teacher's Videotape
- Appendix 13: Comprehension Check Answer Key/Chapter 4
- Appendix 13a: Literary Questions/Chapter 4
- Overhead projector
- VCR/Monitor
- Video camera
- Blank videotape

INSTRUCTIONAL STEPS

1. HOMEWORK
- Collect Literary Question answers.

2. RETELLING ACTIVITY   45 minutes
- Set up video camera.
- Begin taping with student retelling Strophe 1 in front of class.
- Continue taping students signing strophes in order until completed.
- Show their completed, signed version of the strophe immediately.
- Provide individual feedback as each strophe is signed.

3. COMPREHENSION CHECK   **15 minutes**
- Students exchange workbooks.
- Note students who have not completed assignment.
- Display overhead of Comprehension Check Answer Key.
- Students correct each others' answers.
- Students offer explanations for incorrect answers.
- Note any error patterns and address them.

4. LITERARY QUESTIONS   **25 minutes**
- Review Teacher's Videotape, Chapter 4.
- Divide class into four groups.
- Display overhead of Literary Questions.
- Each group discusses questions.
- One leader from each group reports their answer to one question to the class.
- Class discussion of answers.

LITERARY QUESTION GUIDE

1. It tells us that he is very determined and knows what he wants. Also, perhaps the boy is determined to prove his worth by getting a job in the one place that the president of the deaf club said he could not. The boy is desperate to prove to the deaf community that he is important.

2. The boy had to use the visual mode to get the secretary's attention so that he could try and communicate with her. The secretary, being accustomed to the proper mode of discourse in the hearing world, was uncomfortable with the boy's gestures and reacted accordingly.

3. The irony of the boss having an ABC card lies in the fact that the boy's association with the peddler caused him to be thrown out of the deaf club. Moreover, the boy's success in getting a job in the factory that had never hired deaf people before is due to the boss' familiarity with deaf people, due to his association with a peddler.

4. The deaf worker is isolated and not able to socialize with others due to language barriers. The second part of the question is open-ended.

5. ANECDOTE   **10 minutes**
   • Provide anecdote from below or share your own relevant to employment of deaf people
     (e.g., discriminatory practices).
   • Students ask questions related to anecdote.

ANECDOTAL SAMPLE

There was a deaf draftsman employed by a large manufacturing company. Most of his co-workers could not compare with the experience and expertise that this man had in drafting. When the man's boss left his job and his position became available, there was no doubt that he was the most qualified for the position. But because the company feared that he could not talk or use the phone (i.e., they "feared" his deafness), they promoted a much less qualified person to fill the position. The man was extremely disappointed, but accepted their decision. As time went by, the man's new boss was often faced with making decisions that were beyond his level of expertise, so he would always go to the deaf man for help. After forty years of working for the company and never getting his promotion, ironically he was the one who always ended up "supervising" his bosses and continually helping them out. He never did get that promotion.

---

6. NEW HOMEWORK ASSIGNMENT
   • Students to complete Chapter 5, " The Accident."

TOTAL APPROX. TIME ALLOTTED TO CHAPTER 4:   *95 minutes*

Lesson Plan 14

CHAPTER 5		
THE ACCIDENT		
Topic Unit		
13	14	15
Lunch Time	Shortcut to the Cafeteria	The Boy Gets Stuck
Strophes		
48-51	52-55	56-60

Synopsis

The boy becomes aggravated because he cannot hear the bell that sounds for lunch, and he is always last in line, with not enough time to sit and enjoy his lunch. One day he finds a large hole in the floor with gears grinding through it. It leads to the lunch room. The boy decides to use this hole as his shortcut and times his jumps carefully so as not to get caught in the moving gears. He uses this shortcut successfully, until one day, he does not time his jump so carefully, and his shirt becomes entangled in the gears. After hearing his scream, his co-workers turn off the power and call the factory doctor to the scene. The boy is pronounced dead and taken to a funeral home.

MATERIALS/EQUIPMENT NEEDED

- Teacher's Videotape
- Appendix 14: Comprehension Check Answer Key/Chapter 5
- Appendix 14a: Literary Questions/Chapter 5
- Overhead projector
- VCR/Monitor

INSTRUCTIONAL STEPS

1. HOMEWORK
- Collect Literary Question answers.

2. COMPREHENSION CHECK   15 minutes
- Students exchange workbooks.
- Note students who have not completed assignment.
- Display overhead of Comprehension Check Answer Key.
- Students correct each others' answers.
- Students offer explanations for incorrect answers.
- Note any error patterns and address them.

41

3. LITERARY QUESTIONS   **25 minutes**

- Review Teacher's Videotape, Chapter 5.
- Divide class into three groups.
- Display overhead of Literary Questions.
- Each group discusses questions.
- One leader from each group reports their answer to one question to the class.
- Class discussion of answers.

LITERARY QUESTION GUIDE

1. When associated with non-signing people, deaf people have a strong tendency to lose out on what is happening around them. They are left behind, as represented in this episode.

2. Rather than face his problems with communication, the boy prefers to take flight and handle things his own way. Taking matters into his own hands, rather than confronting them and trying to resolve his problems, is the only way he knows.

3. The question is open-ended.

---

4. NEW HOMEWORK ASSIGNMENTS

- Students to complete Chapter 6, "The Second Life."
- Assign one topic unit per student for retelling. If more than 15 students, feel free to assign the same topic unit to more than one student.
- Announce date for Examination #3, which covers the entire narrative as well as comparison between both narratives (See Appendix 15b: Model Examination Sample #3)

TOTAL APPROX. TIME ALLOTTED TO CHAPTER 5:   *40 minutes*

Lesson Plan 15

CHAPTER 6	
THE SECOND LIFE	
Topic Unit	
16	17
The Boy Lives	Return to Work
Strophes	
61-66	67-71

Synopsis

The boy, still very much alive, awakes inside the funeral home, lying next to other corpses. Startled, he jumps out of bed, wraps his naked body in a sheet, and peers through a door into the next room. He sees two men leaning over a body, embalming it. The boy is frightened and runs into the room, alarming the two embalmers. The boy is taken to a hospital, where he spends several weeks with his leg propped up in a cast. He is unable to call and inform his boss of what has happened. When he is released from the hospital, the boy immediately goes to the factory, where he happily surprises his boss and co-workers. After the incident, his boss is so impressed with the hard work and perserverance of deaf people that many more deaf people are hired to work at the factory, including the president of the deaf club.

MATERIALS/EQUIPMENT NEEDED

- Teacher's Videotape
- Appendix 15: Comprehension Check Answer Key/Chapter 6
- Appendix 15a: Literary Questions/Chapter 6
- Overhead projector
- VCR/Monitor
- Video camera(s)
- Blank videotape(s)

INSTRUCTIONAL STEPS

1. HOMEWORK
- Collect Literary Question answers.

2. RETELLING ACTIVITY   45 minutes
- Set up video camera.
- Begin taping students one at a time in a separate room (or two at a time with two cameras) until all students have completed the topic unit level assignment.
- Evaluate students' retelling after class using the Narrative Retelling Evaluation form (Appendix 6b).

3. COMPREHENSION CHECK   15 minutes
- Students exchange workbooks.
- Note students who have not completed assignment.
- Display overhead Comprehension Check Answer Key.
- Students correct each others' answers.
- Students offer explanations for incorrect answers.
- Note any error patterns and address them.

4. LITERARY QUESTIONS   25 minutes
- Review Teacher's Videotape, Chapter 6.
- Divide class into four groups.
- Display overhead Literary Questions.
- Groups discuss questions.
- One leader from each group reports their answer to one question to the class.
- Class discussion of answers.

LITERARY QUESTION GUIDE

1. The fact that the boy is in the morgue shows the irony of doctors and the medical profession and the way they treat and handle the death of a deaf person. It reflects the sometimes shabbiness of the medical profession.

2. It seems that the boy does not confront his problems or ask for help in matters that concern hearing people. However, with deaf people he asks for help. For example, the president of the deaf club was ready to help him until the misunderstanding about the peddler.

3. The boy is thrilled because he triumphed over (and beat) death! It is a big day in his life.

4. The irony lies in the fact that the president told the boy he could not get a job in the factory, yet through the boy's heroics, he ultimately opens up the factory for many deaf employees.

---

5. **INTERVIEW WITH THE SIGNER**   **35 minutes**
   • Show Interview with the Signer in Teacher's Videotape.
   • Class discussion.

6. **NEW HOMEWORK ASSIGNMENTS**
   • Students to write a two-page reaction paper based on the Interview with the Signer.
   • Assign retelling at the chapter level. Students create and retell Chapter 6 with a new ending for the narrative.

TOTAL APPROX. TIME ALLOTTED TO CHAPTER 6:   *120 minutes*

CLOSING LESSON PLAN

MATERIALS/EQUIPMENT NEEDED

- Video camera(s)
- Blank videotape(s)

1. RETELLING   **45 minutes**

- Set up video camera.
- Begin taping students one at a time in a separate room (or two at a time with two cameras) until all students have completed the chapter level assignment.
- Evaluate students' retelling after class using Narrative Retelling Evaluation form (Appendix 6b).

TOTAL APPROX. TIME ALLOTTED TO CLOSING: *45 minutes*

Appendices

Appendix 1

COMPREHENSION CHECK ANSWER KEY

CHAPTER 1 The Eggs

TOPIC UNIT 1: THE FAMILY

Strophe 1
1. On a mountain
2. B

Strophe 2
1. True
2. C
3. True

Strophe 3
1. B

Strophe 4
1. True
2. D

Strophe 5
1. False; two more emerge
2. A

Strophe 6
1. It is not hatching
2. False

Strophe 7
1. False; Mama Eagle watches, too
2. A

Strophe 8
1. Its appearance is different; it has a straight beak
2. C

TOPIC UNIT 2: THE DOCTOR

Strophe 9
1. No
2. False; they call the doctor
3. He flies over

Strophe 10
1. A stethoscope
2. True
3. The beak looks different

Strophe 11
1. The doctor tells them that the baby bird has a straight beak
2. A
3. False; the doctor's diagnosis is inconclusive
4. B

Strophe 12
1. C
2. Distraught, angry
3. They decide to think positive by looking at the fact that they have three normal eaglets

Strophe 13
1. They tuck the eaglets into bed

Appendix 1a

CHAPTER 1 The Eggs

LITERARY QUESTIONS

1) Do you see anything to help establish the time frame of the story?

2) Discuss the irony of the doctor using a stethoscope to examine Straight Beak's beak. What does this particular behavior indicate about the medical profession?

3) Discuss the conflict that began after the hatching of Straight Beak and how it is resolved. What specifically did Mama and Papa Eagle do to each other?

4) What do the eagles symbolize in comparison to the rest of the bird world, including Straight Beak? Discuss the parallel, if any, where the deaf experience is concerned.

Appendix 2

COMPREHENSION CHECK ANSWER KEY

CHAPTER 2 Search for a Cure

TOPIC UNIT 3: THE SOURCE

Strophe 14
1. Mama Eagle
2. False; Papa Eagle awakens
3. True

Strophe 15
1. False; he responds with interest
2. No

TOPIC UNIT 4: THE FAITH HEALER

Strophe 16
1. False
2. True

Strophe 17
1. False
2. No
3. D

Strophe 18
1. B
2. Bald
3. True

Strophe 19
1. To try and turn his beak into an eagle-like beak
2. No

Strophe 20
1. Nothing happens
2. B

Strophe 21
1. False; the preacher gives them a bible
2. True
3. Yes

TOPIC UNIT 5: THE MEDICINE MAN

Strophe 22
1. False
2. False; it is a Native American medicine man
3. Yes

Strophe 23
1. B
2. False; he is sitting
3. A lizard tongue/A rattlesnake's rattle

Strophe 24
1. C
2. Around the fire

Strophe 25
1. C
2. No

Strophe 26
1. C
2. False

TOPIC UNIT 6: THE DOCTORS

Strophe 27
1. Six months
2. No

Strophe 28
1. A

Strophe 29
1. False; they take Straight Beak to several
   more doctors
2. C
3. True

Strophe 30
1. True
2. In response to the stimuli

Strophe 31
1. B
2. Yes
3. They are surprised and cannot believe it

Strophe 32
1. B
2. False
3. True

Appendix 2a

CHAPTER 2 Search For a Cure

LITERARY QUESTIONS

1) What is the common attitude that you detect underlying all the treatments for Straight Beak?

2) How do you know Mama Eagle thinks Straight Beak's condition is severe? Discuss the decision by Mama Eagle to take Straight Beak to several different sources for a cure.

3) What did the Signer imply by repeatedly signing, "Still straight-beaked," in the chapter?

4) Is the recommendation to send Straight Beak to a special school a resolution of the conflict for the parents? How may it or may it not be satisfactory for the parents?

Appendix 3

COMPREHENSION CHECK ANSWER KEY

CHAPTER 3 The School Years

TOPIC UNIT 7:
THE SCHOOL PHILOSOPHY

Strophe 33
1. True
2. True

Strophe 34
1. False
2. An eagle with a shiny bald head
3. A

Strophe 35
1. A
2. No; A. G. Beak Association
3. No

Strophe 36
1. False; the principal explains that the birds can learn how to live like eagles
2. It could change him into an eagle who could live in the eagle world

Strophe 37
1. She is impressed
2. D
3. False; students vary in color

TOPIC UNIT 8: THE LESSONS

Strophe 38
1. True
2. B
3. No

Strophe 39
1. A
2. True
3. False; they stay and watch part of Straight Beak's lesson

Strophe 40
1. False; they leave the lesson while Straight Beak is busy learning
2. False

Strophe 41
1. True
2. B
3. The wings would become stronger and longer (like the eagle's) through stretching

Strophe 42
1. Beak rubbing and wing stretching
2. False; he is ready for high school

TOPIC UNIT 9: THE AMBITION

Strophe 43
1. C
2. False

Strophe 44
1. B

Strophe 45
1. Four (one from Strophe 44)
2. True
3. No

Strophe 46
1. D

Strophe 47
1. True
2. He wants to be a musician
3. D

Strophe 48
1. As eagles
2. Yes
3. To train the birds to hunt like eagles

Appendix 3a

CHAPTER 3 The School Years

LITERARY QUESTIONS

1) What is ironic about the A. G. Beak Association honoring the principal with a plaque? How do you compare the principal's assurances made to Mama Eagle about Straight Beak's education with the earlier attempts to cure Straight Beak?

2) Do you perceive the beak bending and wing stretching exercises as being potentially successful for the birds; and why do you think that Mama Eagle was easily convinced of the merits of these teaching methods for Straight Beak?

3) Why did the remarks that the birds made about their futures infuriate the teacher? Why is hunting being stressed as the only way of life for the birds?

4) Discuss the analogy between the education of Straight Beak and that of deaf children.

Appendix 4

COMPREHENSION CHECK ANSWER KEY

CHAPTER 4 Vocational Training

TOPIC UNIT 10: THE FLYING LESSON

Strophe 49
1. False; they go to a class for vocational training
2. To develop hunting skills like an eagle

Strophe 50
1. False; they are lined up behind the teacher
2. True
3. No

Strophe 51
1. D
2. True

Strophe 52
1. True
2. No

Strophe 53
1. B
2. They take turns
3. Yes

TOPIC UNIT 11: HUNTING LESSON

Strophe 54
1. Head turning for target sighting
2. Sitting

Strophe 55

1. He pulls his wings back at an angle and to the side
2. A rocket

Strophe 56
1. True
2. True

Strophe 57
1. He tilts backwards and brakes
2. A rabbit

Strophe 58
1. No
2. False

Strophe 59
1. No
2. On his back

TOPIC UNIT 12: EVALUATION FOR GRADUATION

Strophe 60
1. False; he is hypocritical in his response to the students
2. True
3. They get stickers (on their foreheads)

Strophe 61
1. Straight Beak's family and other families
2. False

Strophe 62
1. True
2. No

Appendix 4a

CHAPTER 4 Vocational Training

LITERARY QUESTIONS

1) What are the implications of Straight Beak being placed on a vocational track? What would become of Straight Beak if he had stayed on the academic track?

2) Why did the teacher keep praising Straight Beak even though he did not hunt well?

3) Does the attempt by Straight Beak to retrieve the dummy rabbit reflect his competence or the failure of the educational philosophy? Why?

4) Do the graduation ceremony and diploma ensure that the birds are now eagles? How does this philosophy correspond to oralism once prevalent in the education of deaf children?

Appendix 5

COMPREHENSION CHECK ANSWER KEY

CHAPTER 5 Out in the World

TOPIC UNIT 13:
PREPARATION FOR HUNTING

Strophe 63
1. Straight Beak's diploma
2. To go hunting

Strophe 64
1. 4:00 a.m.
2. False; he is impressed
3. C

TOPIC UNIT 14: FINDING PREY

Strophe 65
1. No
2. No

Strophe 66
1. Straight Beak
2. False

Strophe 67
1. A rabbit
2. B

Strophe 68
1. One

Strophe 69
1. No
2. False

TOPIC UNIT 15:
BIRD'S FUTURE CONSIDERED

Strophe 70
1. D

Strophe 71
1. To come with him
2. His carrot

Strophe 72
1. True
2. The carrot
3. Straight Beak is not capable of independence

Strophe 73
1. True

Strophe 74
1. No
2. True
3. What would happen when they died?

Strophe 75
1. False; Papa Eagle calls the brothers to the meeting
2. Yes

Strophe 76
1. He sits and watches television
2. No

Appendix 5a

CHAPTER 5 Out in the World

LITERARY QUESTIONS

1) What does Straight Beak's pleading with the rabbit tell us about his own awareness of his abilities?

2) Compare the experience that the parents were confronted with during Straight Beak's hunting failure to the difficulties they had in his infancy.

3) What does the parents' request of the three brothers to take care of Straight Beak after their death tell us about Straight Beak's place in the eagle world?

4) What do you know about the development of Straight Beak's identity in Part One of the narrative?

Appendix 5b

MODEL EXAMINATION
SAMPLE #1

PART 1

It is suggested that the examination covering this section of *Bird of a Different Feather* should first include Language Notes by choosing 5-10 targeted signs illustrated in the Student Workbook. Each sign should be produced in a created strophe-length event for students to translate into English. Also included should be at least one question developed from the Background sections of the Student Workbook. One example of a Background question is as follows:

> **How do you compare the upbringing of some deaf children with that of Straight Beak? Describe an alternative approach in regards to raising deaf children to ensure more positive post-graduation results.**

Literary Questions should also be included in the examination. Below you will find two examples with corresponding answer guides:

Q- **By the end of Part One, has there been a resolution to the original problem faced by the parents; i.e., has Straight Beak been cured? Why or why not?**

A- No, Straight Beak has not been cured. The parents have overlooked this because their responsibility to find a "cure" was passed on to the school; i.e., the parents expected the school to assume the responsibility of turning him into an eagle. Also, it seems the parents set aside their concerns about the problem instead of facing or confronting it.

Q- **There are some recurring motifs in Part One of the narrative. One example is "still straight-beaked." What is this example's significance in the narrative?**

A- The repetition of "still straight-beaked" implies that a serious disparity remains between the reality of Straight Beak's origins and appearance, and the efforts that both Mama and Papa Eagle have made in raising Straight Beak as an eagle.

Appendix 6

COMPREHENSION CHECK ANSWER KEY

CHAPTER 6 The Bird World

TOPIC UNIT 16:
FAMILY MOVES TO A NEW LAND

Strophe 77
1. B
2. On a different mountain
3. There is plenty of food

Strophe 78
1. Soon
2. D

Strophe 79
1. Papa Eagle
2. No

Strophe 80
1. True
2. No

Strophe 81
1. He is tired
2. He is not supposed to go to the valley
3. His family and school

Strophe 82
1. No
2. No

TOPIC UNIT 17:
SINGING IN THE VALLEY

Strophe 83
1. False

Strophe 84
1. Singing
2. C

Strophe 85
1. No
2. He thinks it is disgusting
3. False

Strophe 86
1. His school
2. C
3. Straight Beak is convinced that he is an eagle

Strophe 87
1. Yes
2. Straight Beak could sing
3. He could not

Strophe 88
1. False; he himself does the demonstration
2. True

Strophe 89
1. False
2. False; Straight Beak becomes completely involved

Strophe 90
1. True
2. No

TOPIC UNIT 18:
BERRIES IN THE VALLEY

Strophe 91
1. He feels indebted to the singing bird
2. Yes
3. A
4. False

Strophe 92
1. He catches him by the tail
2. True

Strophe 93
1. C
2. False

Strophe 94
1. True
2. Berries
3. True

Strophe 95
1. To go eat berries

Strophe 96
1. False; it tastes delicious to Straight Beak
2. Yes

Strophe 97
1. The singing bird's world

Appendix 6a

CHAPTER 6 The Bird World

LITERARY QUESTIONS

1) What do the following: the valley, singing, and eating berries symbolize in terms of the deaf experience?

2) How do you account for Straight Beak's resistance to participate in the bird world?

3) What does the epiphany, "All along I have been imprisoned" mean to Straight Beak? How can he be set free?

4) What problems do you detect that may prevent Straight Beak from "acculturating" with the rest of the birds? How can problems like these be removed for potential members of the deaf community?

Appendix 6b

Story: _____

Part: _____

Name: _____

NARRATIVE RETELLING EVALUATION

SCORE:						COMMENTS

	Understandable		Not Understandable			
1. COMPREHENSIBILITY Is the student's rendition of the narrative understandable? Is pacing used appropriately?						

	Clear		Unclear			
2. SIGN PRODUCTION Are the student's signs produced correctly? Are there deletions of vital signs?						

	Accurate		Inaccurate			
3. USE OF SPACE/CLASSIFIERS Includes correct use of verb agreement, indexing, and classifiers.						

	Full or Adequate		None or Inadequate			
4. NON-MANUAL BEHAVIORS Appropriate and consistent use of facial expressions for syntactic and adverbial markings.						

	Appropriate		Inappropriate			
5. PERSPECTIVE Does the student use the appropriate body shifting and eye gaze to indicate the perspective of the narrator, or of the different characters?						

Score: _____/_____ TOTAL POINTS

Appendix 7

COMPREHENSION CHECK ANSWER KEY

CHAPTER 7 Return to the Eagle World

TOPIC UNIT 19:
EAGLE MOTHER RETURNS

Strophe 98
1. Negative
2. Hide

Strophe 99
1. No
2. C

Strophe 100
1. False
2. D
3. True

TOPIC UNIT 20:
BACK TO THE EAGLE WORLD

Strophe 101
1. No
2. To eat dinner

Strophe 102
1. He hears something coming from Straight Beak's room
2. False; he is sitting
3. "WHAT?!"

Strophe 103
1. Eagles do not sing
2. He would punish Straight Beak
3. No

Strophe 104
1. Every day
2. Time and immersion into the eagle world once again

Appendix 7a

CHAPTER 7 Return to the Eagle World

LITERARY QUESTIONS

1) What does the return to the eagle world imply for Straight Beak?

2) Compare the reaction between Straight Beak and the other birds towards Mama Eagle's landing. Why do you think their responses are different?

3) Has Straight Beak gained any self-identity from his stay in the bird world? Give evidence from this chapter to support your answer.

4) How do you account for Papa Eagle insisting that Straight Beak behave like an eagle, when Straight Beak has failed to acquire "eagle-like" behavior?

Appendix 8

COMPREHENSION CHECK ANSWER KEY

CHAPTER 8 The Operation

TOPIC UNIT 21: THE NEWS

Strophe 105
1. To Straight Beak and his brothers
2. D; the good news is that a doctor is found to help Straight Beak

Strophe 106
1. True
2. Surprised

Strophe 107
1. B
2. Yes

TOPIC UNIT 22: THE CURE

Strophe 108
1. No

Strophe 109
1. An operating room
2. A mask for the anesthesia
3. False

Strophe 110
1. False; it is bandaged
2. C
3. He unwraps the bandage

Strophe 111
1. Mama Eagle
2. C
3. A normal eagle

TOPIC UNIT 23: THE EAGLE FEAST

Strophe 112
1. A party
2. True

Strophe 113
1. False; they said he looks like a parrot
2. D
3. He is confused

Strophe 114
1. B
2. Berries
3. He is full

Appendix 8a

CHAPTER 8 The Operation

LITERARY QUESTIONS

1) What does the parents' support of the operation imply about their acceptance of Straight Beak as an adult?

2) What does the children's mocking of Straight Beak tell us about the difference between children and adults in general? Discuss why adults praise Straight Beak even though he appears more like a parrot than an eagle.

3) What does the parrot symbolize in terms of Straight Beak's involvement in the eagle world?

4) How do you compare Straight Beak's consent to have an operation with that of deaf children undergoing surgery for cochlear implants? Discuss the limitations of cochlear implants and their impact on deaf children.

Appendix 9
COMPREHENSION CHECK ANSWER KEY

CHAPTER 9 The Flight

TOPIC UNIT 24:
RETURN TO THE VALLEY

Strophe 115
1. Visiting his old friends in the valley
2. Dinner time

Strophe 116
1. No
2. Yes
3. "What is wrong with your beak?"

Strophe 117
1. He does not want to appear conceited
2. No

TOPIC UNIT 25:
EJECTED FROM THE CHOIR

Strophe 118
1. No
2. He hears strange sounds
3. False; it is Straight Beak causing the strange sounds

Strophe 119
1. He listens to each bird individually
2. D
3. False

Strophe 120
1. False; he had to sit outside the choir
2. D

Strophe 121
1. A

TOPIC UNIT 26: THE BERRY STRUGGLE

Strophe 122
1. False; all birds are hungry
2. False
3. True

Strophe 123
1. Red
2. They fall down

Strophe 124
1. He turns his head upside down
2. No
3. Yes

TOPIC UNIT 27:
THE FLIGHT INTO SUNSET

Strophe 125
1. D
2. B

Strophe 126
1. The sunset
2. Resolute

Appendix 9a

CHAPTER 9 The Flight

LITERARY QUESTIONS

1) What do the following tell us about Straight Beak's character?
   a) He accepts the idea that he is an "eagle," but he still craves berries.

   b) He thinks the eagle world is superior, but he is anxious to join the choir.

2) In the choice between the bird and the eagle world, how does Straight Beak decide on his fate?

3) How has Straight Beak's identity evolved in Part Two of the narrative?

MODEL EXAMINATION
SAMPLE # 2

PART 2

It is suggested that the examination covering this section of *Bird of a Different Feather* should first include Language Notes by choosing 5-10 targeted signs illustrated in the Student Workbook. Each sign should be produced in a created strophe-length event for students to translate into English. Also included should be at least one question developed from the Background sections of the Student Workbook. One example of a Background question is as follows:

How do you compare the acculturation process that deaf children often undergo with that of Straight Beak? What is the significance of surgery on the acculturation process?

Literary Questions should also be included in the examination. Below you will find several examples with corresponding answer guides:

Q- **In this part of the narrative, Straight Beak experiences two epiphanies. In Chapter 6, he realizes he has been denied his true identity during his upbringing; in Chapter 9, he realizes he must live his own life. What realization did Straight Beak make during his moment of insight before he flew into the sunset in Chapter 9?**

A- Straight Beak went through different stages and much ambivalence before realizing in the end that he did not belong in either of the two worlds in which he was familiar.

Q- **In this narrative, Straight Beak is the protagonist. Who are the antagonists and in what way do they oppose Straight Beak? What is the resulting theme of the narrative?**

A- The principal and doctor oppose Straight Beak because they have authority, expertise and status in society. One does not question their authority or expertise; they are assumed to know what they are doing. Thus, those having a medical/pathological view are considered the antagonists. The resulting theme of the narrative is that despite the medical profession's attempts, they still could not change things which happen within nature.

Q- **Do you like the ending of the narrative? Do you think it is happy or sad? How does your retelling assignment (i.e., your new narrative ending) compare to the original version?**

A- The question is open-ended.

Q- **From whose point of view was the narrative told?**

A- Omniscient author point of view.

Q- **Why does the narrator remind us in the first part that Straight Beak is "still straight-beaked," and not remind us in the second part?**

A- Since the point of view as seen in Part One is from the eagle world, it is important to remind us that the bird is still straight-beaked. However, in Part Two, the narrative's point of view (i.e., focus) changes to more from the Bird world where being straight-beaked is not an issue (except for after Straight Beak's operation).

Appendix 10

COMPREHENSION CHECK ANSWER KEY

CHAPTER 1 Living on the Farm

TOPIC UNIT 1: THE FARM FAMILY

Strophe 1
1. The plains are cold, snowy, windy, and without distinctive features
2. Midwest region
3. True

Strophe 2
1. True
2. Yes
3. The boy is seated and painting

Strophe 3
1. Alcohol breath; bad breath
2. No
3. The mother

Strophe 4
1. Yes
2. The painting and brushes
3. A coat, hat, and scarf

TOPIC UNIT 2: INCIDENT IN THE BARN

Strophe 5
1. False; the boy steps outside
2. It is windy
3. No

Strophe 6
1. False; he has to feel his way around
2. The boy's feet sink into the ground when he steps inside the barn

Strophe 7
1. He feels around until he locates it
2. True

Strophe 8
1. Manure
2. C
3. Many
4. A shovel

Strophe 9
1. False; the window is already broken
2. The boy's paintings
3. The father had used his paintings to cover the windows in the barn

Appendix 10a

CHAPTER 1 Living on the Farm

LITERARY QUESTIONS

1) How does the mood of the protagonist relate to the description of farmland and the inside of the farmhouse?

2) Describe the behavior of the boy and his father as far as communication is concerned?

3) Is there any symbolic relationship between painting and the protagonist's deafness?

4) If you have a hearing friend or relative who happens to have a deaf child and this person does not know any ASL, would you interfere? Why or why not?

Appendix 11

COMPREHENSION CHECK ANSWER KEY

CHAPTER 2 Moving to the City

TOPIC UNIT 3:
MEETING THE DEAF PEDDLER

Strophe 10
1. True
2. False; he stands alone

Strophe 11
1. Mannequins
2. B

Strophe 12
1. C
2. True
3. "Are you deaf?"

Strophe 13
1. True
2. False; the boy catches the peddler

Strophe 14
1. "Where are more deaf people around here?"
2. False
3. False; the peddler disappears

TOPIC UNIT 4:
FINDING THE DEAF CLUB

Strophe 15
1. False; he sits
2. False

Strophe 16
1. True
2. So he can read the address on his paper
3. Yes

Appendix 11a

CHAPTER 2 Moving to the City

LITERARY QUESTIONS

1) With the mood of the city being different from that of the farmland, does the boy feel less isolated? Why?

2) How do you account for the boy's fascination with the shop windows? What do you think the mannequin in the window represents to him?

3) What does the peddler represent for the boy? Do you think the protagonist has a stigmatized image of peddlers?

4) What would you do if you encounter a deaf peddler in the same way as the boy did? Share any experiences you may have had in dealing with peddlers.

Appendix 12

COMPREHENSION CHECK ANSWER KEY

CHAPTER 3 Visiting the Deaf Club

TOPIC UNIT 5:
MEETING THE CLUB MEMBERS

Strophe 17
1. No
2. False; he goes upstairs
3. A

Strophe 18
1. False; the hunchback approaches the boy
2. a) "Are you deaf?"
   b) "Where are you from?"
   c) "What is your name?"
3. Yes

Strophe 19
1. False; he is introduced by the hunchback
2. False

Strophe 20
1. Playing cards
2. A
3. True

TOPIC UNIT 6: THE JOB MARKET

Strophe 21
1. Looking for work
2. D
3. "What kind of jobs are available?"

Strophe 22
1. True
2. High in status

Strophe 23
1. False; the club president asks the printer
2. I.T.U. (International Typography Union)
3. Those jobs are all filled

Strophe 24
1. B
2. Shadow of a beard
3. The sawmill worker's finger is cut off

Strophe 25
1. A
2. False; it is large
3. Deaf people are not hired at the factory

TOPIC UNIT 7:
BANISHED FROM THE DEAF CLUB

Strophe 26
1. The peddler
2. C

Strophe 27
1. True
2. The fact that the boy knows the peddler
3. Because the club president thought the boy was a peddler and not really committed to finding a job

Strophe 28
1. The hunchback
2. No
3. False; the hunchback leaves, too

Strophe 29
1. B
2. To stay at the hunchback's place

Appendix 12a

CHAPTER 3 Visiting the Deaf Club

LITERARY QUESTIONS

1) Describe and contrast the setting and atmosphere of the hallway and clubroom.

2) Discuss the particular questions that the doorman asked the boy. What purpose do you think these questions serve the doorman and the deaf club at large?

3) What does the boy's reaction to the people with power in the club tell us about his character? Describe the image created for the club president based on his physical description and the way he presented himself to the boy.

4) How do you explain the paradox of the club president kicking the boy out of the deaf club, but permitting the peddler to stay?

COMPREHENSION CHECK ANSWER KEY

CHAPTER 4 Getting a Job

TOPIC UNIT 8:
THE AIRCRAFT FACTORY

Strophe 30
1. False; he tosses and turns all night
2. Go to the aircraft factory to get a job
3. The trolley

Strophe 31
1. False
2. False
3. An office

TOPIC UNIT 9: THE JOB REQUEST

Strophe 32
1. True
2. Frightened; startled

Strophe 33
1. He writes on a pad of paper
2. "I want a job"
3. The jobs are all filled

Strophe 34
1. False
2. No; he comes back the next day
3. She just shook her head implying there were no openings

Strophe 35
1. Many times
2. True

Strophe 36
1. Name
2. Sex

Strophe 37
1. Experience
2. True
3. She puts it in a drawer

TOPIC UNIT 10: A JOB FOUND

Strophe 38
1. No
2. She calls the boss on the phone
3. White

Strophe 39
1. True
2. To show that it contained a manual alphabet guide

Strophe 40
1. The boss wants to show him the factory
2. True
3. True

TOPIC UNIT 11: IN THE FACTORY

Strophe 41
1. False; it has many planes
2. B

Strophe 42
1. D
2. True
3. The parts stacked on a rack

Strophe 43
1. True
2. True

Strophe 44
1. True
2. No

TOPIC UNIT 12: THE GOOD WORKER

Strophe 45
1. False
2. D

Strophe 46
1. True
2. Sitting in the cubicle across from the boy
3. No

Strophe 47
1. True
2. False

CHAPTER 4 Getting a Job

LITERARY QUESTIONS

1) What does the boy's persistence at finding employment in the aircraft factory tell us about his character?

2) Describe the cultural conflict created in how the boy tried to get the receptionist's attention. Do you think this accounts for the receptionist's particular behavior towards the boy?

3) What is the irony of the boss having an ABC card?

4) Discuss the differences in the working conditions of the deaf and hearing workers in the factory. If you were the boss yourself, what would you do to improve the working conditions of deaf workers?

Appendix 14

COMPREHENSION CHECK ANSWER KEY

CHAPTER 5 The Accident

TOPIC UNIT 13: LUNCH TIME

Strophe 48
1. B
2. Yes

Strophe 49
1. True
2. Downstairs
3. True

Strophe 50
1. True
2. C
3. No

Strophe 51
1. Yes
2. He gets heartburn and indigestion

TOPIC UNIT 14: SHORTCUT TO THE CAFETERIA

Strophe 52
1. False
2. A shortcut to the cafeteria
3. D

Strophe 53
1. True
2. No

Strophe 54
1. False; he is first in line
2. Yes
3. No

Strophe 55
1. Yes
2. C

TOPIC UNIT 15: THE BOY GETS STUCK

Strophe 56
1. He jumps at the wrong time
2. The shirt on the boy's back

Strophe 57
1. False
2. His face
3. D

Strophe 58
1. Yes
2. False; he is put on the floor
3. True

Strophe 59
1. False
2. He listens to the boy's heart with a stethoscope
3. The boy is pronounced dead

Strophe 60
1. He keeps asking "Why?"
2. True

CHAPTER 5 The Accident

LITERARY QUESTIONS

1) Why is it significant and symbolic that the boy is always the last to know it is lunch time and also the last in line?

2) What does the boy's decision to jump through the shortcut tell us about his character? How do you compare this action with the protagonist running away from home as occurred earlier in the narrative?

3) If you were the boy, what alternative(s) would you consider over jumping through the shortcut? Remember that you are deaf, and the boss can only fingerspell.

Appendix 15

COMPREHENSION CHECK ANSWER KEY

CHAPTER 6 The Second Life

TOPIC UNIT 16: THE BOY LIVES

Strophe 61
1. True
2. Yes
3. A light fixture

Strophe 62
1. A dead body
2. True
3. He is naked

Strophe 63
1. D
2. False; he limps to the door

Strophe 64
1. False
2. The boy starts talking

Strophe 65
1. True
2. The leg is set in a cast to heal
3. C

Strophe 66
1. False; the doctor tells the boy he can leave
2. He uses crutches
3. Yes

TOPIC UNIT 17: RETURN TO WORK

Strophe 67
1. True
2. He hobbles off
3. Yes

Strophe 68
1. The receptionist
2. She screams
3. False

Strophe 69
1. Talking with someone
2. D

Strophe 70
1. D; the boy gestures to explain what happened

Strophe 71
1. The boss hires more deaf people
2. The president of the deaf club
3. True

CHAPTER 6 The Second Life

LITERARY QUESTIONS

1) Why is the boy in the morgue if he is not really dead?

2) How do you account for the pattern of the boy not asking for help (e.g., not asking someone to call the boss from the hospital)? Do you think this pattern also occurs in the protagonist's interaction with deaf people?

3) What is the boy's attitude when he returns to the factory? Why?

4) What is the irony in the fact that the president of the deaf club now works in the aircraft factory?

MODEL EXAMINATION
SAMPLE # 3

It is suggested that the examination covering *For a Decent Living* should first include Language Notes by choosing 5-10 targeted signs illustrated in the Student Workbook. Each sign should be produced in a created strophe-length event for students to translate into English. Also included should be at least one question developed from the Background sections of the Student Workbook. One example of a Background question is as follows:

> **Characterize some of the obstacles facing deaf people in their drive for finding their place in society. What kind of support does the deaf community give to its members?**

Literary Questions should also be included in the examination. Below you will find examples with corresponding answer guides, including questions comparing both narratives:

Q-   What is the main theme of the narrative?

A-   It is a story about independence and the limitations of independence. Also, it is about how perseverance can make your dreams come true, and the notion that individuals have a desire to be a part of a community.

Q-   From whose point of view is the narrative told?

A-   The protagonist; first person point of view

Q-   After reviewing this narrative, discuss what these images foreshadow later in the narrative:
a) The boy struggling through the storm to get to the barn.
b) The stiff, lifeless body of the mannequin in the store window.
c) The sawmill worker's missing finger.

A-   a) Foreshadows his struggle to earn a decent living.
      b) Foreshadows his temporary "death."
      c) Foreshadows his accident.

Q-   **The peddler is a pivotal character. Discuss how his role influences the development of the narrative.**

A-   The peddler contributes to the major changes in the narrative; e.g., if the boy had not met the peddler upon arriving in the city then he would not have found the deaf club. Furthermore, if the boy had not met the peddler, then he would not have been thrown out of the deaf club. Also, the boy got his job in part because his boss had met a peddler and had an ABC card. Thus the peddler indirectly affected all these scenes and had a pivotal role in the narrative.

Q-   **Who is/are the antagonist(s) in this narrative? To what extent do they serve as a contrast to the boy?**

A-   The father (father role), president of the deaf club (who threw out the boy), and the receptionist (gatekeeper role) are all figures with power or have access to power.

Q-   **The narrative appears to be about the boy's struggle to survive in the world. He struggles with two kinds of issues:**
   a) How does he deal with issues that affect his everyday survival?
   b) How does he deal with issues related to his deafness?

A-   If it is an issue dealing with the boy's survival, then he will confront it head on and becoming very assertive. However, if it is an issue dealing with his deafness, rather than confront it, he prefers to side-step it and escape. This shows that the boy has two very differing sides of himself; one associated with survival and assertiveness and the other with deafness and his weak deaf identity.

Q-   **Do you like the ending of the narrative? Is it realistic? How does your retelling assignment (i.e., your new narrative ending) compare to the original version?**

A-   The question is open-ended.

Q-   **Can you identify some common motifs in the two narratives? Find an example of a structural (plot) motif.**

A-   In both narratives, there is a commonality in their escaping and leaving. In *Bird of a Different Feather*, Straight Beak decided at the end of the narrative to leave home; while *For a Decent Living* begins with the boy's decision to leave home. Both narratives show a decision for characters to escape from their present worlds.

Q- What is the common theme that is central to both narratives?

A- The struggle of relationships between self and community; as well as societal expectations versus self–expectations.

Q- How are the protagonists in the two narratives similar? How are they different?

A- The protagonists are similar in terms of deaf identity. In *For a Decent Living,* the character is older than Straight Beak (*Bird of a Different Feather*); however, their self-identity bases are not very high. The characters differ in that the boy (*For a Decent Living*) is more assertive and confrontational (e.g., work-related) than Straight Beak. Straight Beak has a tendency to let everyone control him. This illustrates the point that deaf people can be very different yet still share the same values or state of mind related to their deaf identities.

Q- How are the antagonists in the two narratives similar? How are they different?

A- The antagonists in *Bird of a Different Feather* tend to be involved in the social service and/or human service professions. The antagonists in *For a Decent Living* are more varied and include deaf people themselves. They are similar in that they all have positions of power that can oppress others and insist on instilling their thoughts and ideas on others.

Q- Discuss both characters and their roles as marginal in the societies in which they live.

A- Straight Beak's role throughout the narrative is always marginal; at times he lets himself believe he is an eagle, and at times he lets himself believe he is a bird. This shows that others are always defining who he is and he has not yet made that definition on his own.

The protagonist in *For a Decent Living* knows that he is deaf and feels ashamed about it. This attitude is reflected in his inability to confront hearing people in matters regarding communication problems. Although the deafness is his own problem, the boy tries to avoid dealing with it. Thus his character is not marginal in an obvious way, but there are examples of his marginality throughout the narrative.

YOUR PREMIER SIGN LANGUAGE PUBLISHER

A convenient two-hour self-study for students interested in improving their fingerspelling. A 24-page instructional booklet is included for independent study in the library. Perfect for any level of skill, the videotape is voiced & closed captioned for all kinds of viewers.

Fingerspelling Expressive & Receptive Fluency

by Joyce Linden Groode   ISBN : 0-915035–13–8 $39.95

Using the natural approach of foreign-or second-language teaching principles, *Signing Naturally*, based on the functional-notional approach, is widely used sign language curriculum designed for teaching ASL as a foreign language on almost every major university and college in the United States and Canada. Continuing education and secondary sign language programs have successfully used the *Signing Naturally* curriculum for their students.

Teacher Curriculum Guides of Level 1 and 2 continue to be among some of our best products as instructors realize that the Curriculum Guides include lesson plans, many ready-made classroom materials from which instructors can make transparencies or handouts for classroom use.

For every *Teacher's Curriculum Guide & CRU Videotape* purchased, the instructor will receive a desk copy of *Student Videotext, Workbook and Vocabulary Review* addendum – *Level 1 or 2*. Instructors should send in a filled business reply card attached to their Teacher's Guide.

Teacher's Curriculum Guide - Level 1
by Cheri Smith, Ella Mae Lentz, Ken Mikos
ISBN : 0-915035-07-3 $84.95

Teacher's Curriculum Guide - Level 2
by Cheri Smith, Ella Mae Lentz, Ken Mikos
ISBN : 0-915035-08-1 $84.95

"...it is refreshing to see the wit, humor, cleverness, and gentleness in Baird's art...His art makes us think, analyze, inspect, and examine a deaf individual's approach to life. The ability to do so is a rare skill. You be the judge of the question: *'Why does Chuck Baird create his art?'*"

- Foreword by Deborah Sonnenstrahl

Chuck Baird, 35 PLATES
Text by L.K. Elion   ISBN : 0-915035-18-9 $20.00

order form

BILL TO:
NAME _____

ADDRESS _____

_____

CITY _____ STATE _____ ZIP ____

SHIP TO: (if different)
NAME _____

PROGRAM/DEPT. _____

ADDRESS _____

CITY _____ STATE _____ ZIP ____

PHONE _____ (H/W) please circle

Item #	DESCRIPTION	PRICE	QTY	TOT
2403	Collector's Edition was $19.95	Now 14.95		

SHIPPING RATES -

	WITHIN U.S.A.	ALASKA, HAWAII	CANADA
Orders less than $5.00	add....$1.75	add....$ 6.50	add....$ 5.50
$ 5.00 - $ 24.99	add....$4.25	add....$10.50	add....$ 9.50
$ 25.01 - $ 49.99	add....$5.25	add....$12.75	add....$11.50
$ 50.01 - $ 99.99	add....$6.25	add....$15.75	add....$13.50
$100.01 - $200.00	add....$9.75	add....$18.50	add....$17.50

OTHER COUNTRIES: Please call or FAX for rates.

Subtotal: _____

(for CA residents only) 7.25% sales tax: _____

Shipping & Handling: _____

Total Enclosed: _____

VISA ❑   MASTERCARD ❑   ACCOUNT NUMBER: _____   EXPIRATION DATE: _____

NAME AS SHOWN ON CARD: _____   SIGNATURE (REQUIRED): _____

FL023

DawnSignPress 9080 Activity Road – Suite A, San Diego, CA 92126 V/TDD 619/ 549-5330 FAX 619/ 549-2200

BILL TO:
NAME _____

ADDRESS _____

_____

CITY _____ STATE _____ ZIP ____

SHIP TO: (if different)
NAME _____

PROGRAM/DEPT. _____

ADDRESS _____

CITY _____ STATE _____ ZIP ____

PHONE _____ (H/W) please circle

Item #	DESCRIPTION	PRICE	QTY	TOTA

SHIPPING RATES -

	WITHIN U.S.A.	ALASKA, HAWAII	CANADA
Orders less than $5.00	add....$1.75	add....$ 6.50	add....$ 5.50
$ 5.00 - $ 24.99	add....$4.25	add....$10.50	add....$ 9.50
$ 25.01 - $ 49.99	add....$5.25	add....$12.75	add....$11.50
$ 50.01 - $ 99.99	add....$6.25	add....$15.75	add....$13.50
$100.01 - $200.00	add....$9.75	add....$18.50	add....$17.50

OTHER COUNTRIES: Please call or FAX for rates.

Subtotal: _____

(for CA residents only) 7.25% sales tax: _____

Shipping & Handling: _____

Total Enclosed: _____

VISA ❑   MASTERCARD ❑   ACCOUNT NUMBER: _____   EXPIRATION DATE: _____

NAME AS SHOWN ON CARD: _____   SIGNATURE (REQUIRED): _____

FL023

DawnSignPress 9080 Activity Road – Suite A, San Diego, CA 92126 V/TDD 619/ 549-5330 FAX 619/ 549-2200

PURCHASE POLICY: All orders from individuals must be pre-paid. All orders from schools, libraries and bookstores must be accompanied by payment, a purchase order or other signed authorization. Terms NET 30 days. Write or call for information on Quantity Discounts. Prices subject to change without notice. Please allow 1-2 weeks for processing and shipment of your order (longer for other countries orders). All shipments via UPS. No P.O. Boxes, please.

NOTES: